KU-613-181

Squash

STEPS TO SUCCESS

Contents

Climbing the Steps to Squash Success

Professional squash players have to combine speed, strength, and agility with incredible racket skills. The game today is less a battle of attrition and instead rewards creativity and attacking play. At the recreational level, squash remains one of the most satisfying sports to play and was recently voted the healthiest of sports by *Forbes* magazine. Playing squash well demands a combination of practice, patience, and instruction.

The second edition of *Squash: Steps to Success* brings together the insights of Phil Yarrow, author of the highly acclaimed first edition, and those of former professional player and current teaching professional, Aidan Harrison. Like the first edition, this updated edition focuses on the basics of the game, but it also brings in more advanced concepts, making it applicable to all players, from the beginner to the budding professional.

Squash: Steps to Success has 13 steps that will help you develop basic skills, improve conditioning, vary tactics, and then incorporate all this into match play. The drills at the end of each step are designed to help you practice the skills and ideas discussed in the step. The drills are ordered so that you can first practice the skill or topic in isolation, then under more pressure, and finally in a gamelike situation. Each step features four types of drills:

- *Solo practices*, in which you practice the skill or topic in isolation through continuous repetition.
- *Hitting from a partner's feed*, in which you practice the skill or topic under more pressure. Usually, your partner's feed will be a racket feed to a certain area of the court.

Some drills require your partner to throw the ball. Occasionally, a drill of this type may use two feeders.

- *Two- or three-person routines*, in which you practice the skill or topic in a drill that simulates a game. These drills are designed to be continuous. You should be able to keep the drill going without having to stop to pick up the ball.
- *Conditioned games*, in which you practice the skill or topic in a modified game. These drills require that you use only certain shots or certain areas of the court.

Each drill includes suggestions for increasing or decreasing the level of difficulty so you can progress at your own pace.

The sequence of the steps has been carefully developed to help you quickly achieve a solid squash game built on sound fundamentals. The first four steps teach the basics of swinging and moving around the court. The next six steps outline specific strokes necessary for a solid basic game. The final three steps focus on more advanced topics: preparing yourself mentally and physically for matches and tournaments, adapting tactics to your opponent's play, and improving your fitness so that you can compete at higher levels.

Get ready to climb a staircase, one that will lead you to become an accomplished squash player. You can't leap to the top; you get there by climbing one step at a time. Progress through the steps as quickly or as slowly as you like, but remember that to become a good squash player you must develop a strong basic game and correct court movement.

Each of the 13 steps is an easy transition from the one before. As you progress, you'll develop your skills and learn to maneuver your opponent around the squash court. As you near the top of the staircase, you'll become more confident in your ability to challenge higher-level players in league or tournament play or just for fun.

Follow the same sequence each step of the way:

1. Read about what the step covers, why the step is important, and how to execute or perform the step's focus, which may be basic skills, ideas, tactics, or a combination of the three.

2. Follow the photographs to learn exactly how to position your body to execute each basic skill. Each skill has three general parts: preparation (getting into a starting position), execution (performing the skill that is the focus of the step), and follow-through (reaching a finish position or following through to the starting position).

3. Review the missteps—common errors that often occur—and the recommendations for correcting them.

4. Perform the drills to improve your skills through repetition and purposeful practice. Read the directions for each drill, including the success checks. Practice accordingly and record your score. Drills are arranged in an easy-to-difficult progression to help you achieve continual success.

At the end of each step, have a qualified observer such as a teacher, coach, or trained partner evaluate your technique. This subjective evaluation of your basic technique or form will help you use correct form to enhance your performance. Record your scores, and make sure you have sufficiently mastered the step before moving to the next step.

Enjoy your step-by-step journey to developing your squash skills, building confidence, experiencing success, and having fun.

Acknowledgments

We would like to thank Phil's wife, Ginger Yarrow, for all her help with the countless rough drafts of this book. Also, we would like to thank Alex Melkonian, Amber Kirchens, Brandon Flores, Dana Betts, and Katherine Massey for modeling for the photographs, as well as Harrow Sports for providing the clothing and equipment.

The Sport of Squash

Not enough time in your life to play a sport regularly? Do you have time in your schedule only to do a boring, repetitive workout that lacks competition and mental stimulation? Think again. Playing squash develops speed, endurance, agility, coordination, and court savvy, yet the average length of a match between two recreational players is less than 40 minutes. Squash is one of the fastest and most athletic sports. The popularity of the sport is due in large part to the intensely competitive workout it generates in such a short time. It's the perfect sport for busy people. Over 15 million men and women in 122 nations now enjoy squash, and the numbers are increasing rapidly.

The beauty of the game is that it's simple to learn yet difficult to master. All you do is hit a small ball against the front wall of a room so that it is out of reach of your opponent. The challenge, of course, is achieving this goal against the more skilled opponents you'll play as you improve. The game can be physically and mentally draining, but at the end of the match, you'll be satisfied, exhilarated, and probably a little tired.

DEVELOPMENT OF SQUASH

For centuries people have played games that involve hitting a ball with a racket, either against a wall or back and forth to each other across a net. The most common example is tennis. In the 19th century the popularity of sports involving rackets and balls led to the creation of the game *rackets* in the Fleet Prison in London, England. The prisoners exercised by hitting a small, hard ball around the walls of a large room. Ironically, the game later became popular in English public schools.

It was at one of these schools, Harrow School in London, where squash is believed to have originated around 1830. Students, waiting to get on to the rackets court, began practicing in a smaller area by hitting a soft rubber ball against the wall. They found that playing with the softer ball produced a wider variety of shots and required much greater effort. The name of the game came from the ball's "squashiness" as it hit the walls.

In the early years of the sport there was little standardization. Many slight variations of the game were seen. Fortunately, only two variations became popular. Most of the world played with a soft ball on 21-foot-wide (64 m) courts, whereas North Americans played with a hard ball on slightly narrower courts.

The rules of the soft-ball version of the game were finally formalized in 1923, and the number of squash players soon overtook that of its parent game, rackets. The growth areas for squash at this time were in countries where British forces were stationed. People in India, Pakistan, Egypt, South Africa, Australia, and New Zealand began to learn the game. In 1930, the first British Open was held, and it was considered the first unofficial World Championships. An Englishman, Don Butcher, won the event, beating fellow Englishman Charles Read in a best-of-three match series. For the following 35 years players from Egypt and Pakistan dominated top-level squash. Many of these players learned the game as ball boys for uncovered courts. They had limited coaching but plenty of time to practice. They developed techniques that involved exotic shot making and became extremely proficient at the game.

In the late 1960s, Jonah Barrington, a rugged, determined Irishman, finally broke the Egyptian and Pakistani domination. Barrington didn't begin playing squash until his early 20s, but he showed an unparalleled dedication to the game. His rigorous training took him to a fitness level far above that of the top players of the day. Barrington won the British Open six times, proving that fitness could prevail over shot making.

Squash would never be the same again. Barrington pushed all the top professionals to work hard on their fitness. The players that followed in Barrington's footsteps all possessed remarkable speed, stamina, and strength besides incredible racket skills. Three players stand out: Australia's Geoff Hunt and Pakistan's Jahangir Khan and Jansher Khan. Hunt was the best of a number of strong players who emerged in the 1970s from Australia. He took over from Barrington as the number one player in the world. Jahangir Khan is widely regarded as the greatest ever to play the game. His aggressive style overwhelmed opponents. He was so dominant that at one stage, during the 1980s, he went five and a half years without losing a single match. Jansher Khan, no relation to Jahangir, was finally able to combat Jahangir's strength by skillfully varying the pace of matches.

In the late 1980s and early 1990s, certain modifications were made to the game at the professional level to encourage more attacking play and to try to make the matches more exciting for spectators. The first modification was to reduce the height of the tin by 2 inches from 19 inches (48 cm) to 17 inches (43 cm). This made it easier for players to hit winners and thus encouraged attacking play rather than long, drawn-out defensive rallies. The second modification was to switch from traditional scoring to 9 points to point-per-rally scoring to 15 points. The scoring system was later modified again to point-per-rally scoring to 11 points in which a player must win by 2 clear points. The change in the scoring system was due to the increasing length of matches in professional tournaments. Under the traditional scoring system, in which points are only scored when a player is serving, it was not uncommon for matches to last in excess of 2 hours. A typical professional match now usually lasts 30 to 70 minutes. This has led to players being fresher at the latter stages of tournaments, which has resulted in better-quality semifinal and final matches.

These changes to the professional game switched the advantage back to the more offensively minded players from those that base their games primarily on fitness. But in today's game all the top players have incredible fitness and mobility. The two standouts from the recent era are Canadian Jonathan Power and the Scottish-born Englishman Peter Nicol. These two shared center stage in the squash world for almost a decade starting in the mid-1990s. Both players recently retired, paving the way for the incredibly talented Egyptian Amr Shabana to take over the top spot. The professional game today is extremely competitive, and Shabana is tested by a host of other players, including Egyptians Ramy Ashour and Karim Darwish, Englishmen James Willstrop and Nick Matthew, and the Frenchman Gregory Gaultier, which makes tournaments week after week exciting and unpredictable.

In North America the squash scene has changed rapidly in recent years. Squash, as most of the world knows it, was played in North America only recreationally, in the summertime. In the winter tournament season, the exclusively North American game known as hard-ball squash, played on narrower courts with a hard, solid ball, was the sole game. In the early 1990s, though, the popularity of the international soft-ball version of the game began to take over. Today, most players in North America play soft-ball exclusively, throughout the year.

The hard-ball and soft-ball games require different techniques and strategies. The hard ball travels faster around the court and thus requires quicker reflexes. The rallies tend to be short, and the ability to hit winners is essential. The soft ball also travels at high speeds but slows as it rebounds off the walls and floor. Players must run more in the soft-ball game, but they have more time to play their shots. Winning shots are harder to come by in soft-ball. Rallies are longer, and to win points, a player must use a combination of shots to work the opponent out of position. These differences made the conversion from the hard-ball game difficult for many long-time squash enthusiasts in North America.

The problem was initially compounded by the lack of experienced soft-ball coaches to help these players make the necessary changes to their games. Recently, however, many experienced coaches have moved to North America.

The number of professional tournaments in North America has increased dramatically and thus has led to several professional players basing themselves in the United States or Canada. The college game is now exclusively soft-ball, and junior squash in the region is improving in leaps and bounds. This book focuses exclusively on the soft-ball version of the game.

Despite its ever-growing popularity around the world, squash has suffered from underexposure because of the difficulty in viewing games. In the past, the audience could see matches only from balconies above the back wall of the court, severely restricting the number of spectators. In the 1970s, however, glass back walls were introduced, soon followed by fully transparent portable courts for major events, with one-way-view glass walls. These courts can be erected in large halls, allowing spectators to be seated around the court and to watch from all angles. Audiences of over 3,000 people can now attend these events.

Nevertheless, with two players hitting a small, fast-moving ball in an enclosed room, squash has proved to be an extremely difficult sport to televise. Recent innovations in this area, however, have opened up opportunities. Besides the glass courts, which allow a variety of camera angles, colored walls and white balls have helped make television viewing easier. These improvements, along with a new generation of high-definition television cameras, have made the ball easier to follow on a television screen. These developments may allow greater exposure for the sport in the future.

MATCH PLAY

Squash is played by two people on a court 32 feet (9.75 m) long and 21 feet (6.4 m) wide (figure 1). After a 5-minute warm-up, the players decide who will serve first by spinning a racket. The ball is put into play by a serve, and a rally is played out. A player wins a rally when the opponent either hits the ball into the tin (a metal strip 19 inches [48 cm] high at the bottom of the front

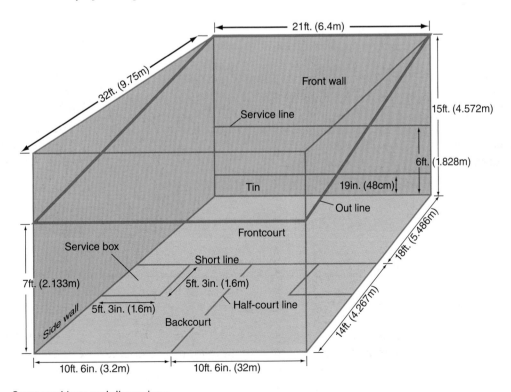

Figure 1 Court markings and dimensions.

wall), hits above the out-of-court lines, or doesn't reach the ball before it bounces twice. During the rally the player may hit the ball on the fly or after it has hit the floor and may use the side and back walls to maneuver the ball onto the front wall.

Most squash matches used to use the traditional (international) scoring, in which a player scores points only when serving, and each game is played to 9 points. Point-per-rally (or American) scoring, however, has now taken over as the dominant scoring system. In point-per-rally scoring, the player winning the rally scores a point regardless of who served, and each game is played to 11 points.

Normally, a player wins a match by winning three out of five games. Occasionally, matches are won by winning two out of three games.

A match can involve two teams of players. Normally, each team consists of three or five players. The top players on each team (known as the first string) play each other, the second-best players (second string) play each other, and so on down the team. A team scores a point for each match won.

A tournament involves a number of players or teams competing against each other. Most tournaments are single elimination—a player or team losing a match is eliminated from the tournament. Some tournaments, however, are double elimination. A player or team must lose twice before being eliminated. Another kind of tournament is the round-robin tournament, in which the player or team plays all the other players or teams in the tournament. The winner of the tournament is the player or team recording the most wins.

SQUASH RULES

When the players step on court, they have 5 minutes to warm up before the first game begins. During the warm-up the players stand on opposite sides of the court and hit the ball against the front wall so that it rebounds to their opponent. After 2 1/2 minutes of the warm-up the players switch sides of the court. The warm-up serves two purposes: it gives the players an opportunity to practice their strokes, and it allows them to warm up the ball. A squash ball is cold at first and doesn't bounce much. Once the players begin to hit it, the ball becomes warmer and begins to bounce more. The ball should be warm before the players start the first game.

After the warm-up the players spin a racket to decide who will serve first. Similar to tossing a coin, one of the players chooses a distinguishing feature on the racket, such as the logo on the butt of the racket handle, to be pointing up or down or to the right or left. The other player spins the racket. If a correct call was made, that player gets to choose whether to serve. If an incorrect call was made, the player who spun the racket gets the choice instead. Nearly always the player chooses to serve, particularly with traditional scoring in which a player can score only when serving.

Serving

The player serving first can decide whether to serve from the left or right service box. Normally, players serve from the right service box against right-handed opponents and from the left service box against left-handed opponents. They do this so they can serve to their opponent's backhand side, which is often the weaker side.

The server must have at least one foot inside the service box when contacting the ball. Part of the foot can be off the floor, but none of the foot can be touching any of the lines forming the service box.

The server throws the ball in the air and hits it before it hits the floor, directly onto the front wall. The ball must strike the front wall above the service line and below the out line. It must then rebound to the opposite back quarter of the court. If the receiver hits the ball on the fly (i.e., before it bounces on the floor), the serve is good. If, however, the receiver allows the ball to bounce before hitting it, the ball must bounce within the back quarter of the court for the serve to be good. The opposite back quarter is the area enclosed by the short line, half-court line, side wall, and back wall, on the opposite side of the court from which the server served. (Note: Hitting the short line or the half-court line isn't considered a good serve.) The ball may hit the side wall, the back wall, or both walls before striking the floor as long as it strikes the walls below the out line. An unsuccessful service is called a fault, and the receiver immediately wins the rally. The following is a list of all possible types of faults:

- The server doesn't have at least one foot in the service box at the point of contact (foot fault).
- The server hits the ball after it hits the floor.
- The server swings and misses the ball.
- The ball fails to hit the front wall above the service line.
- The ball hits one of the side walls before hitting the front wall.
- The ball bounces outside the opposite back quarter of the court.
- The ball hits the front, side, or back wall above the out line.
- The server hits the ball twice.
- The server is struck with the ball after it rebounds from the front wall.

Winning a Rally

Once the server has completed the service, the service line and all the lines on the floor play no further part in the rally. The only boundaries now are the out lines and the tin.

Besides winning a rally when your opponent is unsuccessful with a serve, you win a rally if your opponent

- fails to hit the ball before it bounces twice,
- fails to hit the ball against the front wall,
- hits the ball into the tin,
- hits the ball onto the floor before it hits the front wall,
- hits the ball onto any of the walls on or above the out line,
- hits the ball onto the ceiling or against or through any fittings hanging from the ceiling,
- carries the ball on the racket strings or hits the ball twice,
- touches the ball with anything other than the racket,

- deliberately interferes with your shot, or
- accidentally interferes with your shot to such an extent that you're impeded from making a possible winning shot. (This is discussed further in the section Lets and Strokes.)

Scoring

The squash world has shifted toward using point-per-rally scoring, in which a point is scored regardless of who served. In fact, all men's and women's professional matches now employ point-per-rally scoring, and many national organizations now recognize this as their official scoring method. Point-per-rally scoring is played to 11 points. There are no tie-breaks, but instead a player must win by at least 2 clear points.

The traditional scoring system in which games are played to 9 points and points are scored only by the server is still used for some matches. If the receiver wins the rally, the score doesn't change; but the receiver gains the serve for the next rally. If the game score reaches 8-8, a tie-break is used. The player who reached 8 points first is the receiver and chooses either *set one* to play the game to 9 points, or *set two* to play the game to 10 points. Usually, the receiver chooses set two, because choosing set one immediately gives the server *game ball,* which means that the server is one rally away from winning the game. The player who is one rally from winning the match is at *match ball.*

When the score is called, the server's points are always called first. For example the score 3-5 means that the server has 3 points and the receiver has 5 points. If both players have the same number of points (e.g., 3-3), the score is called as *3 all.* If a player has zero points, the term *love* is used. Therefore, at the beginning of each game the score is *love all.*

SAFETY

Two players moving rapidly around a small room have a high risk of injury from running into each other or hitting each other with the ball or racket. For this reason both players must always be aware of the position of their opponent. The responsibility for safety during a rally lies with both the striker (the player about to hit the ball) and the nonstriker (the player who has just hit the ball). The nonstriker should make sure the striker has a direct line to move to the ball and has room to make a full swing at the ball. Crowding your opponent is not only hazardous to your health, but also unsporting.

When striking the ball, you should be aware of exactly where your opponent is so that you minimize the risk of injuring your opponent with the racket or the ball. Think about trying to control your racket as you swing; avoid particularly an excessive follow-through. If you feel there is the possibility of hitting your opponent with either your racket or the ball, stop and ask for a *let* (i.e., for the rally to be replayed).

One of the most dangerous situations that can occur is when you turn on the ball. This is when you are in a back corner and the ball bounces off the side wall and the back wall out toward the center of the court. Instead of backing up toward the center of the court to allow room to hit the ball, you make a 180-degree turn and hit the ball on the opposite side of your body. This is dangerous because as you turn you can't see your opponent. Your opponent has no idea where you're going to hit the ball and doesn't know where to move to avoid being hit. If this situation occurs, *always* stop before hitting the ball and request a let.

LETS AND STROKES

To promote safety in a match, the rules provide for a system of *lets* and *strokes*. This complex system includes many gray areas as to whether a let or a stroke (penalty point) should be awarded.

In considering lets and strokes, keep two main points in mind: safety and fairness. Safety is of prime importance. If a player discontinues playing a shot because of a genuine concern about hitting an opponent, the player is entitled to at least a let as long as he could have made a good return. Beginners often start off playing lets whenever there is any interference. This certainly increases safety. But you also want to consider what is fair. Sometimes the player who was stopped had such a clear advantage that he would almost certainly have won the rally if not for the interference of the opponent. Often, the opponent has made every effort to avoid the interference, but it was caused by his own poor shot. In this situation the opponent deserves to lose the rally. So when a player stops, the hypothetically fair outcome should be considered. If a player who clearly had the upper hand stops because the opponent was in the way, the fair outcome is to award a stroke.

To give you a greater understanding of the rules regarding lets and strokes, we'll consider three common occurrences on a squash court. While reading the following, remember two things: if your opponent's actions were a deliberate act to interfere with your shot, you're always entitled to a stroke; and if you wouldn't

have been able to make a good return, the decision should always be a *no let* (i.e., you lose the rally).

You Hit Your Opponent With the Ball

The rules state that once your opponent has struck the ball, you must have the entire front wall to aim at. Therefore, if you hit your opponent with the ball, the decision about whether to award a let or a stroke depends on whether the ball was traveling directly toward the front wall. If it was, you are entitled to a stroke because your opponent failed to give you the whole of the front wall to aim at. If the ball was traveling toward the side or back wall, a let should be played.

Deliberately striking your opponent with the ball is dangerous and reflects poor sporting behavior. If you're in a situation in which you think you may strike your opponent, refrain from hitting the ball. The rules apply in the same way as if you had hit the ball and had struck your opponent. If you would have struck your opponent with a shot going directly toward the front wall, you're entitled to a stroke. If you would have struck your opponent with a shot going toward the side or back wall, the decision is a let.

The only exception to these rules is if you turn on the ball. Under no circumstance can you be awarded a stroke if you turn on the ball, regardless of whether you hit your opponent or would have hit your opponent with a shot traveling directly toward the front wall. Whenever you find yourself turning on the ball, you should stop and a let should be played. *Turning on the ball* refers not only to when you make a 180-degree turn in the back corner, but also to when you allow the ball to travel around your back or when you hit the ball between your legs or behind your back.

Your Opponent Impedes You From Reaching the Ball

The rules state that, after striking the ball, your opponent must give you direct access to the ball. If your opponent impedes your direct access to the ball, the decision about whether to award a let or a stroke depends on whether you were stopped from playing a possible winning shot. So it depends largely on how good your opponent's shot was. If it was a good shot and you would have only been able to keep the ball in play, you're entitled to a let. If it was a poor shot and you would have had a good opportunity to hit a winner, you're entitled to a stroke.

The rules also state that you must make every effort to reach the ball. This prevents you from claiming a let at the slightest sign of interference when you see that your opponent has hit a good shot or when you're too tired to run for the ball. However, you don't have to crash full speed into your opponent to claim a let. You should stop before making significant contact.

Your Opponent Doesn't Give You Enough Room to Swing at the Ball

The rules state that your opponent must give you complete freedom to play any shot you choose. If your opponent crowds you and inhibits your backswing or your follow-through, you're entitled to a stroke as long as you could have played a shot directly to the front wall. If you could have hit a shot only to the side or back wall, you're entitled to a let only.

Besides being awarded for interference, lets are also awarded in these situations:

- When the ball breaks during a rally
- When the receiver isn't ready and makes no attempt to hit a serve
- When there is a distraction on or off the court

ROLES OF THE MARKER AND REFEREE

Traditionally, in top-level events, a marker and a referee normally officiate matches. The *marker* is responsible for the following:

- Announcing the match to the spectators
- Calling the score
- Calling service faults, down (the ball hitting the tin), out, and not up (any other failure to make a good return)
- Repeating decisions made by the referee

The *referee* is responsible for the following:

- Making decisions on appeals for lets
- Making decisions on appeals against the marker's calls
- Correcting any errors made by the marker (e.g., with the score)
- Keeping track of the time during the warm-up and between games (players are allowed a 90-second break between games)

Increasingly, in top-level matches there has been a move to have three officials. A referee sits in the middle behind the glass wall and performs all the duties of a marker. The two side judges sit behind the back wall close to each back corner. If a player appeals for a let, each official makes a decision at the same time as to whether it should be a let, stroke, or no let. The final decision is based on the calls by the majority of the officials. If each official has a different view, the referee's decision is final.

Sometimes, particularly in club matches, a single official performs the duties of both the referee and the marker. When you play recreationally, most of the time you officiate your own matches. In this situation the server should call the score before serving to reduce the chances of a conflict over the score. Players must agree about whether interference warrants a let or a stroke. This can lead to many disputes, which more often than not result in playing a let. You should remember, however, that not offering your opponent a stroke when you know she deserves one or taking a let when you couldn't have made a good return is cheating.

If you feel you deserve a let or a stroke, appeal to the referee, or to your opponent if you have no referee. The correct way to appeal is to call out "let, please." You should never ask for a stroke. The referee, or you and your opponent mutu-ally, will decide the correct award. Remember that you must appeal at the time of the incident. Appealing a few shots later or at the end of the rally about interference or some kind of distrac-tion isn't permitted. It will be considered that you played through the interference, and you won't be awarded a let.

This limited interpretation of the rules is a good basis from which to start. As you become a more experienced player, particularly if you begin to play in tournaments, you must study the rules in greater depth. For the complete rules of squash, visit the World Squash Federation's Web site at www.worldsquash.org.

SELECTING EQUIPMENT

You can buy squash equipment from most major sports stores or from the pro shop at your squash club.

Rackets

Squash rackets range in price from U.S. $60 to $200. The important aspects to consider when choosing a racket are weight, racket-head size, and stiffness. If you are just beginning and don't want to spend too much money on a racket, you should be able to find a suitable racket at the lower end of that price range. As you play more, you may find that a more expensive racket improves your game.

A squash racket (figure 2) is similar to a racquet-ball racket except that it has a longer shaft. Until the early 1980s, most squash rackets were made of wood. Wooden rackets tended to be quite heavy and flexible; that is, the shaft would bend slightly if the racket head and handle were pulled in the same direction. This flexibility caused a whip as the player swung at the ball, which many players liked at the time because it increased the power of the shot. In the 1980s, however, more players began to use rackets made of graphite. These rackets were lighter, and the racket frames were stiffer. The weight difference added significant extra power to shots, and the stiffness increased control. Graphite rackets gave players such a noticeable advantage that within just a few years wooden rackets became practically obsolete.

The move to graphite rackets was fol-lowed by increases in the size of the racket head. Players found that larger racket heads increased the size of the racket's sweet spot—the area of the racket face where the player gains maximum power with the least vibra-tion. The larger sweet spot was particularly good for beginners, who had more chance of hitting the ball with power.

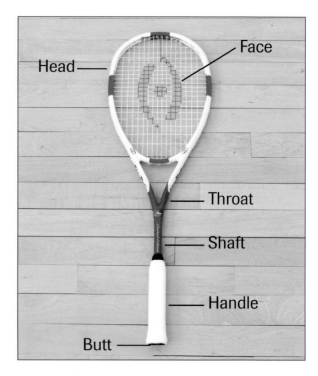

Figure 2   Squash racket.

Today, we are seeing moves toward even lighter, stiffer rackets with larger racket-head sizes, but this kind of racket may not be the best type for you. Try out as many rackets as possible before buying one. In general, you can swing lighter rackets faster, creating more power. This is only true, however, if you have a good swing. If you're just learning the game and don't consistently swing well, too light a racket could reduce your power. Rackets range from about 130 to 200 grams and can be head heavy, evenly balanced, or head light.

A racket with a little flexibility can help increase power in your shots, but the trend today is definitely toward the control offered by stiffer frames. Beginners should look for a racket with a large racket head. Often, the same racket is made in several head sizes, with the size of the head quoted in square centimeters. The largest head size is generally 525 square centimeters. A racket with a head of this size gives the beginner more power and reduces the chances of mis-hitting the ball. Because a large head size causes a loss in control, however, a more experienced player will probably want a midsize head in the range of 470 to 500 square centimeters.

Balls

A squash ball is a hollow rubber ball about 2 inches (5 cm) in diameter. Squash balls come in a variety of speeds. Dunlop is the most popular brand of squash ball; however, Prince, Wilson, and Black Knight also make balls used in tournament play. The slowest ball is the Dunlop Pro ball, which is a black ball with two yellow dots. This is the official ball of the World Squash Federation and both the men's and women's professional tours. The Dunlop Pro ball is used for most tournament play. The Dunlop Competition ball is a black ball with a single yellow dot. It is slightly faster than the Pro ball and hangs in the air 10 percent longer. It is good for club-level play. The Dunlop Progress ball is a plain black ball. It hangs in the air 20 percent longer than the Pro ball and is good for beginner-level players. Finally, the Dunlop Max ball is a blue ball. It is 12 percent larger than the Pro ball and hangs in the air 40 percent longer. It is an excellent ball for kids to use when they are first learning the game.

Squash balls last for a limited amount of time. An old ball will often break; the rubber splits and the ball no longer bounces consistently. Even if it isn't broken, you shouldn't use a ball that has become shiny and starts to skid on the floor or off the walls.

Eyewear

In the United States players are required to wear eyewear when playing squash, and juniors must wear eyewear in all tournaments worldwide. Many players find this to be a nuisance because in the middle of a hard game eyewear can feel uncomfortable and the lenses can fog up, leading to restricted vision. The increase in safety, however, easily outweighs the inconvenience. The squash ball is the perfect size to fit into the eye socket. Being hit in the eye with the ball can do serious damage and can even cause blindness.

Choose eyewear that is light but strong enough to withstand a blow from either the ball or the racket. Eyewear ranges in price from U.S. $20 to $100. At the top level, Rudy Project eyewear is the most popular. It is in the higher end of the price range, however, and may not be the best choice for players just taking up the game. Other companies, such as Harrow, make lower-cost eyewear, which is more than adequate for most players.

You shouldn't wear eyewear without lenses or with glass lenses. If you wear glasses anyway, you probably won't want to wear your regular glasses, even if they have plastic lenses. The frames are unlikely to be strong enough to protect from a blow from your opponent's racket. You can buy sports glasses that can be fitted with your prescription lenses, or you can buy protective glasses that you can wear over your regular glasses.

If you have a problem with the lenses fogging up, try wearing a headband to reduce the moisture accumulating above your eyes.

Footwear

Squash shoes (figure 3) are similar to shoes worn in other indoor sports such as racquetball, volleyball, and tennis. For regular players a pair of shoes may last only a couple of months. Often, the toe wears down before the rest of the shoe because it slides along the floor as you stretch for shots. Shoes with leather toes can reduce this problem, but be wary of the added weight. Make sure that the soles of your shoes are nonmarking. You should never wear running shoes with black soles on the squash court. The soles leave ugly black marks on the floor that are difficult to remove.

Comfort and durability are major factors in deciding which squash shoes to buy, but along with this you should consider weight, the grip on the sole, and the support the shoes give. The shoes should be lightweight so you can move quickly, have a strong grip so you feel confident that you won't slide when stretching, and give enough support so you can twist and turn without spraining an ankle.

Don't skimp on buying shoes (squash shoes run anywhere from U.S. $40 to $130) because you may end up paying for it with a serious injury.

Apparel

Squash apparel is similar to that for racquetball and tennis. When squash was played predominantly in private men's clubs, strict rules applied

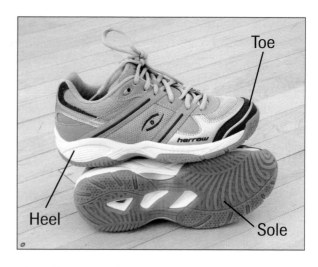

Figure 3 Squash shoe.

to apparel. Only collared shirts were allowed, and clothes had to be white. Recently, with squash becoming popular with more people, many of the old rules have been considerably relaxed. Even in major tournaments colored clothing is normally allowed as long as it is deemed appropriate for squash. (Beach shorts and tank tops would probably be ruled out!) Some of the major tournaments still require players to wear collared shirts. Otherwise, T-shirts are normally as acceptable as collared shirts.

Apparel is probably the least important item of equipment you buy for squash. As long as you're comfortable, clothing will have little effect on your game, although some people believe that looking good gives them a little more confidence.

GETTING STARTED

Now that you have a little background on the game, all you need to do is find a court. Traditionally, squash was played primarily by wealthy men in private men's clubs. In many countries the game grew in popularity in the 1970s and 1980s, and many stand-alone squash facilities were built. In the United States, squash received a boost in the 1990s as a number of players switched from playing racquetball to playing squash. This spurred many health club owners to

convert racquetball courts to squash courts or to build squash courts in new complexes. Besides health clubs, many universities and some YMCAs have squash courts.

If you're not sure where you can play in your area, contact your local or national squash association. Most local and national squash associations can easily be found on the Internet. The following is a list of contact information for selected squash organizations:

World Squash Federation: www.worldsquash.org

European Squash Federation: www.europeansquash.com

U.S. Squash: www.ussquash.com

England Squash: www.englandsquash.com

Squash Australia: www.squash.org.au

Professional Squash Association: www.psa-squash.com

Women's International Squash Players Association: www.wispa.net

Key to Diagrams

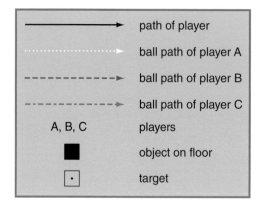

⟶	path of player
⋯⋯⟶	ball path of player A
– – –⟶	ball path of player B
– – –⟶	ball path of player C
A, B, C	players
■	object on floor
⊡	target

Proper Grip and Basic Swings

Squash is one of the fastest sports in the world. The ball often moves at speeds of more than 100 miles per hour (161 km/h). Although the ball loses pace as it rebounds off the front wall, players are often standing only 10 feet (3 m) or so from the front wall and must react quickly. Professional squash players appear to have almost superhuman reactions. The key is the way they grip and handle the racket, which allows them to prepare almost instantaneously for either a forehand or backhand shot.

The grip is difficult to master, especially if you've been playing squash for a while with an incorrect grip. So don't be surprised if the correct grip feels unnatural at first and your grip moves as you hit the ball. Keep working with it, periodically checking to make sure it's correct. In the long run the correct grip will come to feel more comfortable and will greatly improve your shot production.

Once you learn to grip the racket properly, the next step is to develop a basic forehand and backhand drive. A drive is a shot hit after the ball has bounced on the floor. A forehand drive is hit from the side of your body on which you hold the racket. A backhand drive is hit from the opposite side of your body. You'll need to be prepared to hit forehand and backhand drives from all areas of the court.

Most beginners find the forehand swing easier than the backhand swing at first because its motion is similar to the one used when hitting a baseball or swinging a golf club. The motion, in fact, is almost identical to that of trying to skim a stone across water. As you begin to practice the correct swings, however, you'll probably find that the motion on the backhand side is more natural.

DEVELOPING THE CORRECT GRIP

The way you grip the racket is important for good stroke production. The correct grip enables you to keep the racket face open—that is, facing slightly upward. This in turn makes it easier to slice drop and kill shots and hit shots out of the back corners.

Novice players often grip the racket so that when they swing, the racket face is closed—that is, facing directly at the front wall or downward. This often gives them more power but diminishes control and makes it difficult to hit in the backcourt.

Try to use the same grip for both forehand and backhand drives because the speed of the game normally doesn't allow enough time for grip changes. Grip the racket as if you were shaking hands with it (figure 1.1a). Your thumb and index finger should make a V running down the top inside edge of the racket (i.e., the top left edge for right-handed players, the top right edge for left-handed players). Curl your index finger around the racket handle and leave a gap between the index finger and the other three fingers (figure 1.1b). Gripping the racket with the fingers too close together tends to lead to a lack of control over the racket face. Try to grip the racket handle firmly enough to make sure the racket won't fly out of your hand as you hit the ball but not so tightly that it causes tension in your hand or forearm. It's best to start off by gripping the racket about halfway up the racket handle. Gripping higher on the handle (choking up) helps with control, but you lose power; the reverse is true when you grip lower on the racket handle.

Figure 1.1   Grip

1. Grip racket as if shaking hands with it
2. Make V with thumb and index finger along inside edge of racket
3. Leave gap between middle and index fingers
4. Keep racket face open

a

b

Misstep
The racket slips while hitting shots.

Correction
Grip the racket a little tighter.

Misstep
Your hand becomes tired from hitting shots.

Correction
Don't grip the racket quite so tightly.

HANDLING THE RACKET

Improving your racket handling will help you prepare quickly for your shots, giving you more time to concentrate on your swing and on where to hit the ball. Early preparation is the key to timing your strokes well and moving smoothly on the court. By being ready early, you'll have many options about where to hit the ball, thus making your shots harder to read.

Try to keep your wrist cocked so that the racket is at a 90-degree angle to your forearm (figure 1.2). The racket face should be open. Hold the racket face steady. You should feel as if you always have total control over the racket face. As you wait for your next shot, concentrate on keeping the racket face from dropping toward your feet. Keep it up at least level with your racket hand. While preparing for your shot, make sure your wrist is firm. The racket face should not move around too much. Being aware of the exact location of your racket face will help you avoid rushing your shots and will give you the maximum amount of control over your shots.

Figure 1.2   Handling the Racket

1. Cock wrist
2. Keep racket face up

Misstep
Your shots lack control.

Correction
Make sure you keep your wrist firm throughout the shot.

Misstep
You feel rushed on shots.

Correction
Keep your wrist cocked so that the racket face is always up, and make sure that you prepare the racket early for your shots.

Usually, it is easy to diagnose grip or racket handling problems. The trick is making the corrections. The correct way often feels unnatural at first, so you need to check yourself constantly until it becomes habitual to do it the right way.

Grip and Racket Handling Drill 1.
Roll Ball Around Racket Face

Make sure you grip the racket in the correct manner. Hold the racket out in front of you. Turn your wrist so that your knuckles are facing down and the racket face is parallel to the floor (figure 1.3). Place the ball on the racket strings and roll it around the racket face for as long as you can before it falls off. Then twist your wrist so that your knuckles and the other side of the racket face are facing up and repeat the exercise.

To Increase Difficulty

- Do the exercise with your eyes closed.
- Walk around the court while doing the exercise.

To Decrease Difficulty

- Choke up on the racket.
- Keep the ball moving at a slower pace or not at all.

Success Check

- Keep the racket face parallel to the floor.
- Move the ball at a controlled pace.

Score Your Success

60 seconds or more without ball falling off racket face (knuckles down) = 5 points

30 to 59 seconds without ball falling off racket face (knuckles down) = 3 points

Figure 1.3   Roll ball around racket face, knuckles down.

29 seconds or less without ball falling off racket face (knuckles down) = 1 point

60 seconds or more without ball falling off racket face (knuckles up) = 5 points

30 to 59 seconds without ball falling off racket face (knuckles up) = 3 points

29 seconds or less without ball falling off racket face (knuckles up) = 1 point

Your score ___

Grip and Racket Handling Drill 2.
Bounce Ball on Racket Face

Hold the racket as you did in Grip and Racket Handling Drill 1, but this time bounce the ball on the racket face as many times as you can (figure 1.4). As you do, try to maintain the proper grip.

To Increase Difficulty

- Bounce the ball higher in the air.
- Walk around the court while bouncing the ball on the racket face.

To Decrease Difficulty

- Choke up on the racket.
- Use any grip necessary to keep the drill going.

Success Check

- Keep a firm grip.
- Use a short, controlled, punchy movement with the racket face.

Score Your Success

20 bounces or more in a row = 5 points

10 to 19 bounces in a row = 3 points

9 bounces or fewer in a row = 1 point

Your score ___

Figure 1.4 Bounce ball on racket face.

Grip and Racket Handling Drill 3.   *Racket Blocks*

Stand about 15 feet (4.6 m) from a partner with your racket face up, holding your racket in front of your body. Have your partner throw balls alternately to each side of your body. Stop the ball with your racket face, letting the ball fall to the floor and roll back to your partner. Attempt 10 blocks.

To Increase Difficulty

- Have your partner throw randomly to either side of your body.
- Have two partners throw to you to increase the speed of the drill.

To Decrease Difficulty

- Have your partner throw the ball more slowly.
- Have your partner throw only to one side.

Success Check

- Hold the racket firmly.
- Keep your wrist cocked.
- Watch the ball onto the racket face.

Score Your Success

8 to 10 successful blocks = 5 points

6 or 7 successful blocks = 3 points

3 to 5 successful blocks = 1 point

Your score ___

Grip and Racket Handling Drill 4.   *Racket Catches*

Stand about 6 feet (1.8 m) from a wall. Throw the ball against the wall, and then catch it on your racket face. Try to cradle the ball with your racket face as you do when you catch a ball with your hands and pull it into your chest. By moving the racket face down as you catch the ball, you'll prevent it from bouncing off the strings. Attempt 10 catches.

To Increase Difficulty

- Have a partner hit the ball onto the wall for you to catch on your racket face.

To Decrease Difficulty

- Throw the ball in the air and catch it on your racket face.

Success Check

- Cradle the ball with the racket face.
- Watch the ball onto the racket face.

Score Your Success

5 to 10 successful catches = 5 points

3 or 4 successful catches = 3 points

1 or 2 successful catches = 1 point

Your score ___

EXECUTING THE FOREHAND SWING

Many people find that they can pick up a squash racket for the first time and hit the ball quite hard on the forehand side. But building the necessary accuracy into the forehand shot is often difficult. For this reason it's important to learn the basic elements of the swing. These elements apply to all forehand shots, regardless of whether you're in the backcourt, in the frontcourt, attacking, or defending.

When hitting the ball on the forehand, keep in mind that the power comes from the backswing, not the follow-through. To achieve this, you must try to position yourself so that your front shoulder is turned toward the side wall and your back is almost facing the front wall (figure 1.5a). Your front foot should be closer to the side wall than your back foot. Hold your racket high, with your elbow away from your body and bent at no more than a 90-degree angle. Cock your wrist so that you hold the racket face almost directly above your head.

The swing is a U-shaped swing: bring the racket face down, through the ball, and then up on the follow-through in one continuous motion (figure 1.5, b and c). Try to make contact with the ball to the side of your front foot. Keep your arm straight and your wrist cocked so that the racket face is at the same level as your hand. Keep the racket face open on contact so that you can hit up through the ball. It's important to keep your wrist firm throughout the shot so that you push through the ball rather than snap your wrist. Your hips will start off facing the back corner and will turn slightly toward the side wall on the backswing, but as you make contact with the ball and follow through, they should stay still and be facing the side wall at the end of the swing. You should be getting the power in the shot from your shoulders, not from your wrist or hips.

Misstep
The ball goes down the middle of the court.

Correction
You hit the ball too far forward; wait longer and try to hit it to the side of your front foot.

Make sure that you prepare your racket early, but try to avoid stepping across with your front foot too soon. The step should come just before you begin the swing, and you should bend your leading leg so that you transfer your weight to the front foot as you begin the backswing. Bring the racket face through the ball quickly to generate power in the shot, but don't try to hit the ball too hard. Keep the swing relaxed, and put your effort into bending down to the ball rather than trying to muscle it with your body.

Keep your eyes fixed on the ball throughout the shot, and try to hit the ball at a comfortable distance from your body. Don't hit the ball at the top of the bounce; by letting it start to drop, you'll find it much easier to hit the ball up and send it into the back corners.

As you swing through, drop your front shoulder and position your body in a crouched position so that your head is over the ball (figure 1.5, d and e). Make sure you keep your head still throughout the swing and stay as balanced as possible.

Misstep
Your shot lacks enough power to reach the back wall before bouncing twice.

Correction
Make sure you start with the racket up high on the backswing and your shoulder turned so that your back is almost facing the front wall. Bring the racket face through the ball more quickly, but try to keep your body still. Make sure that you time the step into the shot with your front foot just before you begin the swing.

Figure 1.5   Forehand Swing

a

PREPARATION

1. Prepare racket early and high
2. Cock wrist
3. Bend elbow
4. Watch ball
5. Step across on front foot
6. Drop front shoulder and point it toward side wall

b

FORWARD SWING

1. Keep transferring weight onto front foot
2. Bend leading leg
3. Turn hips toward side wall
4. Let ball begin to drop before making contact

CONTACT

1. Contact ball to side of front foot
2. Keep racket face open
3. Keep wrist firm and cocked

c

(continued)

Figure 1.5 (continued)

FOLLOW-THROUGH

1. Keep hips still
2. Keep weight on front foot
3. Don't slide or lift back foot off ground

d

FINISH

1. Turn head to watch ball
2. Bend elbow
3. Bring racket face up to front shoulder

e

Misstep
The ball goes into the side wall.

Correction
Either the ball got too far behind you or, more likely, you moved your hips toward the front wall as you made contact and followed through.

EXECUTING THE BACKHAND SWING

Unlike the forehand, the backhand is often very difficult for the beginner at first. If the player can make contact at all, it can seem nearly impossible to hit a backhand shot with any power. Players who don't learn the basic principles of the backhand swing will constantly find it the weak part of their game. Their opponents will be looking to seize any chance to hit the ball to the backhand side of the court, forcing many errors and poor returns.

If you learn and practice the basic components, however, you'll find that the backhand swing is a natural motion. These rudiments will improve all your backhand shots.

As with the forehand, the power on the backhand comes from the backswing, not the follow-through. Again, you must try to position yourself so that your front shoulder is turned toward the side wall and your back is almost facing the front wall (figure 1.6a). Having your front foot closer to the side wall than your back foot will facilitate your body positioning. Your racket face should be behind the back of your neck, and your racket hand must be close to your back shoulder. Keep your wrist cocked and firm so that your racket face is steady before you swing. Your elbow should be in quite close to your body and should be pointing downward, not toward the side wall. This will make it much easier to get your shoulders into the shot.

As you swing, the racket face will again follow a U shape, coming down on the backswing, through the ball, and then up on the follow-through (figure 1.6, b and c). Try to make contact with the ball to the side of your body a few inches (or cm) forward from your front foot. Keep your arm straight and your wrist cocked so that the racket face doesn't drop below the level of your hand. Make sure, again, that your racket face is open as you make contact with the ball and that you keep your wrist firm, pushing through the ball instead of snapping your wrist. Your hips will turn from facing the back corner at the start of the backswing to facing the side wall as you strike the ball. Again, keep your hips still as you make contact and follow through.

The timing of the shoulder turn, your step into the shot, and the swing is crucial to hitting with power and control on the backhand. Try to think about it in three stages. First, prepare your racket early (when you see it's going to be a backhand), and begin to turn your body so that you face the side wall. Then, as the ball approaches, slowly begin to turn, drop your front shoulder, and pull your elbow back around your body so that you are getting a good windup for the shot. Finally, after the ball has bounced, step across with your front foot and swing through. Make sure that the swing comes immediately after the step, that you bend your leading leg, and that you keep your weight on the front foot throughout the shot.

Misstep
The ball hits too low on the front wall.

Correction
Make sure the racket face is open. On the forehand, check that your thumb and index finger are making a V along the top inside edge of the racket. On the backhand, make sure you don't turn your wrist inward. Bend your knees more and keep your wrist firm throughout the swing.

The racket face needs to come through the ball quickly to generate power in the shot, but again, don't try to muscle the shot with your body. Relax as you swing, and put your effort into bending down. Don't let your back foot slide or lift off the ground as you strike the ball. Also, try to keep your head still. Again, watch the ball constantly and try to hit the ball at a comfortable distance from your body. As with the forehand, let the ball begin to drop from the top of its bounce before you strike it so that it will be easier to hit up through the shot.

Bend your elbow on the follow-through, and bring the racket face up so that it finishes almost above your head (figure 1.6, d and e). Keeping your body still and controlling your racket face on the follow-through will not only improve the accuracy of your shots but also keep you from having an excessive, dangerous swing that could injure your opponent.

Figure 1.6   Backhand Swing

a

b

c

PREPARATION

1. Racket face close to back of neck
2. Wrist cocked
3. Knuckles facing up
4. Elbow in close to body
5. Elbow pointed downward
6. Step across on front foot
7. Position body to face back corner

FORWARD SWING

1. Drop front shoulder and point it toward side wall
2. Move elbow back around body
3. Keep transferring weight onto front foot
4. Bend leading leg
5. Let ball begin to drop before making contact

CONTACT

1. Contact ball slightly forward of front foot
2. Keep racket face open
3. Keep wrist firm and still cocked

d

e

FOLLOW-THROUGH

1. Keep hips still
2. Keep weight on front foot
3. Don't slide or lift back foot off ground

FINISH

1. Turn head to watch ball
2. Bend elbow
3. Bring racket face above head

Misstep
You completely miss the ball.

Correction
Keep your eyes on the ball as you swing, and take your time.

Forehand and Backhand Swings Drill 1. *Shadow Swings*

Practice forehand and backhand swings in front of a mirror. Check to make sure that you're using a high backswing, and try to avoid snapping your wrist as you follow through. If you don't have a large mirror, you can try watching yourself in the glass back wall of a squash court. Complete 50 swings, alternating between forehand and backhand.

To Increase Difficulty

• Close your eyes and practice your swing.

To Decrease Difficulty

• Break down the swing into stages—backswing, contact, and follow-through—and practice each stage separately.

Success Check

• Keep your elbow away from your body on the backswing.
• Use a U-shaped swing.
• Transfer your weight onto your front foot as you swing.

Score Your Success

50 alternating forehand and backhand swings = 5 points
Your score ___

Forehand and Backhand Swings Drill 2. *Hit Shots Past the Short Line*

Position yourself about halfway between the front wall and the short line and about 5 feet (1.5 m) from the side wall. Stand with your racket prepared and your body facing the side wall. Throw the ball against the side wall so that it bounces about 4 feet (1.2 m) away from you and directly between you and the side wall. When it bounces on the floor, step across with your front foot, turn your front shoulder toward the side wall, and then swing through. Try to hit the ball straight so that it stays close to the side wall and deep enough so that it bounces past the short line (figure 1.7). Hit 10 forehand shots, and then hit 10 backhand shots.

To Increase Difficulty

• Hit the ball deeper in the court.
• Hit the ball above the service line.
• Hit crosscourt toward the opposite back corner.

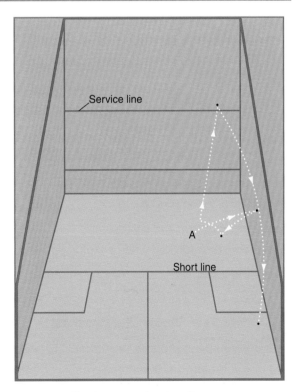

Figure 1.7 Hit shots past the short line.

To Decrease Difficulty

- Concentrate only on making contact; don't worry about where the ball goes.

Success Check

- Prepare your racket before throwing the ball.
- Throw the ball so that it bounces in line with your front foot.
- Aim high on the front wall.

Score Your Success

8 to 10 forehand shots bounce past the short line = 5 points

6 or 7 forehand shots bounce past the short line = 3 points

3 to 5 forehand shots bounce past the short line = 1 point

8 to 10 backhand shots bounce past the short line = 5 points

6 or 7 backhand shots bounce past the short line = 3 points

3 to 5 backhand shots bounce past the short line = 1 point

Your score ___

Forehand and Backhand Swings Drill 3. *Target Drives*

This drill is similar to Forehand and Backhand Swings Drill 2, except you should stand on the short line and try to hit the ball so that it bounces on a target placed against the side wall about 2 feet (0.6 m) behind the back of the service box (figure 1.8). Attempt 10 forehand shots and 10 backhand shots.

To Increase Difficulty

- Vary the pace of your shots.
- Hit crosscourt shots at a target in the opposite back corner.

To Decrease Difficulty

- Make the target area larger.
- Concentrate solely on making good contact with the ball.

Success Check

- Time your step and swing to increase power.
- Swing through fast while keeping your body still.
- Avoid snapping your wrist.

Score Your Success

5 to 10 forehand shots hit the target = 10 points

3 or 4 forehand shots hit the target = 5 points

1 or 2 forehand shots hit the target = 1 point

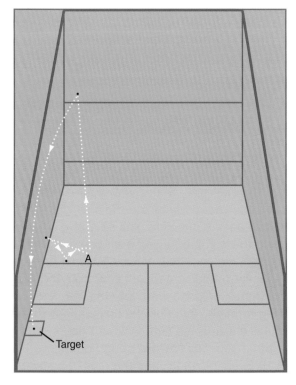

Figure 1.8 Target drives.

5 to 10 backhand shots hit the target = 10 points

3 or 4 backhand shots hit the target = 5 points

1 or 2 backhand shots hit the target = 1 point

Your score ___

Forehand and Backhand Swings Drill 4.
Hit Shots From Partner's Drop

Stand on the T and have a partner stand to your side about 6 feet (1.8 m) away. Your partner drops the ball about 2 feet (0.6 m) away from you (figure 1.9). Let the ball bounce, reach the top of its bounce, and start to drop. Then swing and hit a straight drive toward the back corner. Hit 10 shots using a forehand swing and 10 shots using a backhand swing.

Figure 1.9   Hit shots from partner's drop.

To Increase Difficulty

- Aim higher on the front wall.
- Alternate straight and crosscourt drives.
- Set a target to aim at.

To Decrease Difficulty

- Shorten your backswing and concentrate only on striking the ball.

Success Check

- Watch the ball.
- Bend your knees.
- Keep your head still as you swing.

Score Your Success

8 to 10 forehand shots bounce behind the short line = 5 points

6 or 7 forehand shots bounce behind the short line = 3 points

4 or 5 forehand shots bounce behind the short line = 1 point

8 to 10 backhand shots bounce behind the short line = 5 points

6 or 7 backhand shots bounce behind the short line = 3 points

4 or 5 backhand shots bounce behind the short line = 1 point

Your score ____

Forehand and Backhand Swings Drill 5.
Hit Shots From Partner's Feed

Have a partner stand in the back corner and hit short shots to the front of the court. From the T, step across toward the ball and hit straight drives to the back corner, keeping the ball close to the side wall (figure 1.10). Try to keep the shots no farther from the side wall than the width of the service box. If possible, your partner should keep the drill going without stopping between shots. Hit 10 forehand shots and 10 backhand shots.

To Increase Difficulty

- Have your partner feed lower shots, forcing you to bend more.
- Set a target in the back corner to aim at.

To Decrease Difficulty

- Have your partner feed higher shots.
- Have your partner stop after each shot so you have time to prepare for the next one.

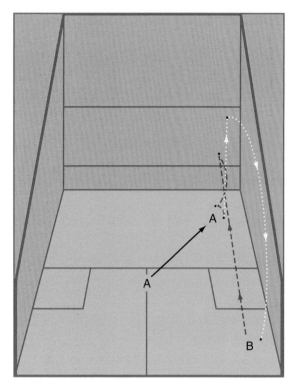

Figure 1.10 Hit shots from partner's feed.

Success Check

- Watch the ball as your partner strikes it.
- Don't get too close to the ball.
- Push through as you make contact.

Score Your Success

10 consecutive forehand shots bounce past the back of the service box = 10 points

7 to 9 consecutive forehand shots bounce past the back of the service box = 5 points

4 to 6 consecutive forehand shots bounce past the back of the service box = 1 point

10 consecutive backhand shots bounce past the back of the service box = 10 points

7 to 9 consecutive backhand shots bounce past the back of the service box = 5 points

4 to 6 consecutive backhand shots bounce past the back of the service box = 1 point

Your score ___

Forehand and Backhand Swings Drill 6.
Crosscourt Rallies

Stand near the back of the service box on one side of the court. Have a partner stand near the back of the service box on the opposite side. Throw the ball against the side wall closer to you. After it has bounced on the floor, hit the ball against the front wall so that it rebounds toward your partner (figure 1.11). Your partner then hits the ball back to you. Keep the rally going as long as you can. To hit the ball so that it travels across the court to your partner, make contact slightly farther forward from your front foot and aim for the middle of the front wall. Make sure that you hit forehands on the forehand side and backhands on the backhand side (i.e., move toward the middle of the court so that you can hit the ball between your body and the side wall closer to you).

To Increase Difficulty

- Stand farther back in the court.
- Increase the number of consecutive shots by 10 until you reach 50 consecutive shots.

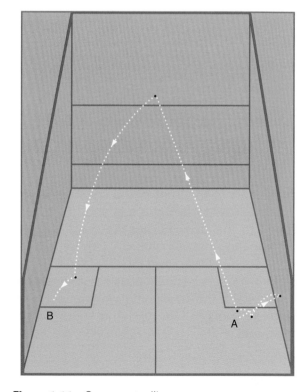

Figure 1.11 Crosscourt rallies.

Success Check

- Hit slightly forward from your front foot.
- Prepare your racket early.
- Aim at the center of the front wall.

Score Your Success

20 consecutive shots = 10 points

15 to 19 consecutive shots = 5 points

10 to 14 consecutive shots = 1 point

Your score ___

SUCCESS SUMMARY OF PROPER GRIP AND BASIC SWINGS

Achieving the correct grip on the racket is difficult, but it's the key to good shot production. Always pretend you're shaking hands with the racket so that you form a V with the inside edge of the racket. Remember not to grip so tightly that you strain your wrist or forearm, but to keep your wrist firm throughout the shot. Always keep your wrist cocked and the racket face open.

Developing a solid basic swing is fundamental because all other swings are based on it. Remember to prepare your racket early, keep your wrist cocked, bend your knees, and keep your trunk and feet still as you swing through the shot. Swing through quickly, but concentrate on generating power from your shoulders, not your hips. And, of course, always keep your eye on the ball.

Once you've completed the drills in this step, ask a partner to check your fundamentals using the photos in figures 1.1, 1.2, 1.5, and 1.6.

Before moving on to step 2, Court Movement, evaluate how you did on the drills in this step. Tally your scores to determine how well you have mastered the correct grip, racket handling, and forehand and backhand swings. If you scored 75 points or more, you are ready to move on to step 2. If you did not score at least 75 points, practice the drills again until you raise your scores before moving on to step 2.

Grip and Racket Handling Drills

1. Roll Ball Around Racket Face	___ out of 10
2. Bounce Ball on Racket Face	___ out of 5
3. Racket Blocks	___ out of 5
4. Racket Catches	___ out of 5

Forehand and Backhand Swings Drills

1. Shadow Swings	___ out of 5
2. Hit Shots Past the Short Line	___ out of 10
3. Target Drives	___ out of 20
4. Hit Shots From Partner's Drop	___ out of 10
5. Hit Shots From Partner's Feed	___ out of 20
6. Crosscourt Rallies	___ out of 10
Total	___ *out of 100*

Now that you have mastered the grip and the basic forehand and backhand swings, it is time to start working on court movement. Step 2 will introduce you to how to move to each area of the court as efficiently as possible and in such a way that you are best positioned to play your shot. You will learn the difference between *traditional* movement, in which you strike the ball with your front foot forward, and *dynamic* movement, in which you strike the ball off your back foot. The step will teach you the best time to use each type of movement.

Court Movement

Some top players move so gracefully around the court that they make the game look effortless. You'll soon find out, if you haven't already, that squash is rarely effortless. What is the secret to this seeming contradiction? Certainly the hours of hard physical training that top players put in is one reason. But that isn't all; their knowledge of correct court movement is just as important.

Now that you understand basic swings, it's time to look at the way you move around the court. Good court movement will bring together all aspects of your basic game. You'll be able to position yourself better for shots. You'll also be able to cover your opponent's shots quickly and thus have more time to play your own.

TRADITIONAL AND DYNAMIC MOVEMENT

Good court movement is important for two main reasons. First, it allows you to cover the court quickly and efficiently. Second, it helps you to position yourself well for shots. Players who haven't developed good movement constantly find themselves out of position, rushing madly around the court trying to keep the ball in play. It's often such an effort to get to the ball that it's difficult to think about anything else, such as stroke production and strategy. These players improve only slowly, if at all, because in game situations they're never in control of their shots and thus can never work on improving their strokes.

If you work on court movement, you'll soon find that your poise, balance, power, and composure on court improves. Smooth movement will eventually become second nature, and you'll then be able to concentrate on executing your strokes and developing good basic strategy.

It is important to keep movements as smooth and as unhurried as possible. Balance is key. Keep on the balls of your feet, ready to move in any direction to retrieve your opponent's shot. If you're in a reasonable position watching your opponent strike the ball, you'll nearly always have plenty of time to retrieve the shot. So don't rush. Take your time and concentrate on moving to a sideways position a reasonable distance from the ball.

Misstep
You are too close to the ball to swing properly.

Correction
Don't rush at the ball. Take your time and concentrate on moving smoothly.

Good movement consists of a combination of quick, short steps; shuffle steps; and long strides to the ball. Your movement should be similar to that of a boxer: Stay balanced with little shuffles before taking a big step when going for the punch. Start with a split step on the T to get you on the balls of your feet in a balanced position ready to move in any direction to the ball. Then take small steps or shuffles to move in the direction of the ball. Finish with one or two large steps to efficiently cover the court and put yourself in the best position for your shot.

For the most part, try to hit shots off your front foot; this is known as *traditional* movement (figure 2.1). At times, however, it will be easier and more efficient to hit the ball off your back foot, which we call *dynamic* movement (figure 2.2). On the backhand side it is critical to turn your front shoulder toward the side wall. Because leading with your front foot makes this shoulder turn more easily, try to use traditional movement on the backhand side whenever possible. On the forehand side, it is best to hit off your front foot when you have plenty of time and can easily transfer your weight to the front foot as you hit the ball. Therefore, in general it is preferable to use traditional movement when moving to the front of the court or if you are in the back corner and are waiting for the ball to bounce back off the back wall. If you are quickly stepping to the side or are reaching back for a forehand, it is more efficient to use dynamic movement and hit off the back foot. Also, if you are at full stretch moving forward on the forehand, you can typically reach forward farther with the racket if you lead with your back foot instead of your front foot.

Figure 2.1 Traditional movement in which the shot is hit off the front foot.

Figure 2.2 Dynamic movement in which the shot is hit off the back foot.

SPLIT STEP

After hitting the ball, try to move back to the middle of the court to prepare for your next shot. From the middle of the court, you can cover all four corners. If your last shot was to the frontcourt, it is best to stand right up on the T so that you can cover your opponent's shot back to the front. If you hit the ball to the back court, it is best to recover to a position about 2 feet (0.6 m) behind the T. From here you should still have time to cover a shot to the front-court, and you will not get caught too far forward if your opponent hits a shot to the backcourt.

Ideally, you should be at the middle of the court just as your opponent is about to hit the ball. As your opponent strikes the ball, perform a split step. A split step is a little bounce or hop that puts you on the balls of your feet with your feet about shoulder-width apart and your knees very slightly bent (figure 2.3). The split step will help you quickly get your momentum going in whatever direction necessary so that you can explode onto your opponent's shot.

| **Figure 2.3** | **Split Step** |

1. Feet shoulder-width apart
2. Knees slightly bent
3. Balanced on balls of feet

Misstep
You are too slow off the mark to the ball.

Correction
Take a quick bounce or hop on the T to get into split step position, balanced on the balls of your feet. Constantly watch the ball.

FRONTCOURT MOVEMENT

When moving in the frontcourt, you should use traditional movement as much as possible because this will help you get your body in the best position to hit the ball. Dynamic movement, however, can be helpful on the forehand side if you are under pressure. It allows you to stretch farther and thus return a shot that you might not be able to reach using traditional movement.

When moving in the frontcourt, move from the T to the ball in a slight J shape, rather than straight at the ball, to help you get into a sideways position to play the shot (figure 2.4). Begin with a split step followed by small steps so that you maintain balance. Then take a couple of large steps into the shot. Try to time your movement forward so that your second-to-last step is with your back foot. Pivot on your back foot, turning your front shoulder toward the side wall and preparing the racket. Your final step with your front foot should come just before your swing. After hitting the ball, push back off your front foot and backpedal directly to the T as long as this doesn't impede your opponent from moving directly to the ball.

Figure 2.4   Traditional Frontcourt Movement

1. Move in J shape
2. Pivot on back foot
3. Step across on front foot
4. Push off front foot
5. Backpedal to T

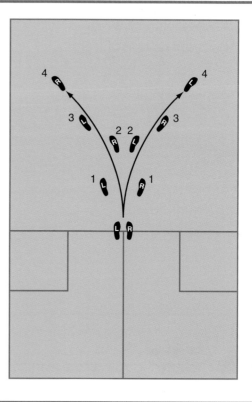

Use dynamic frontcourt movement only on the forehand side and only when you are under pressure and forced to stretch for the ball. In these situations, however, take your last step with your back foot rather than your front foot, and hit from an open stance position because you will be able to reach farther. If possible, still try to turn your shoulders toward the side wall just before striking the ball. After your split step, move forward with a series of small steps to keep balanced, and then take a couple of large steps to the ball (figure 2.5).

Because you are under pressure and need to move quickly to the ball, move directly toward it rather than in a J shape. This time make your second-to-last step with your front foot and take a final large step toward the ball with your back foot. Use a shorter backswing than normal, but make sure your racket is up before you take that last step so you can swing as soon as your leading foot hits the ground. Push off the leading foot directly back to the T, making sure not to impede your opponent's path to the ball.

Figure 2.5 | **Dynamic Frontcourt Movement**

1. Move directly to ball
2. Last step is long stride to ball with back foot
3. Turn shoulders to side wall before striking ball
4. Step back toward T

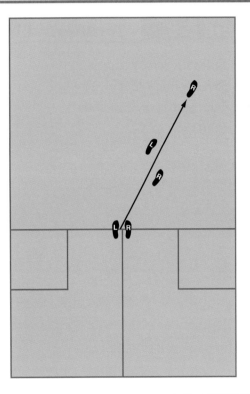

Misstep
You are incorrectly positioned to swing properly, leading to mis-hits or lack of power on your shots.

Correction
When using traditional movement, be sure to use a J-shaped path to the ball. Use dynamic movement on the forehand side if you are under pressure.

MIDCOURT MOVEMENT

Movement in the midcourt is usually the easiest. Normally, you don't need much more than a shuffle and a step to get into position to hit the ball. You can use either traditional or dynamic movement in the midcourt on the forehand side, but you should always try to use traditional movement on the backhand side. Use traditional movement on the forehand side if the ball is coming to you slowly enough so that you can get your front foot across and step forward to the shot. If the ball is coming quickly at you, dynamic movement will likely be easier than traditional movement on the forehand side.

When using traditional midcourt movement, after your split step, move sideways from the T with a shuffling or sidestepping motion (figure 2.6). This will allow you to stay balanced and make it easier for you to make final adjustments to get into good hitting position. When moving to the side, one side step usually is enough. Pivot on your back foot again to get the front foot across. Step slightly forward into the shot to generate power. After hitting, step directly back to the T.

Figure 2.6   Traditional Midcourt Movement

1. Sidestep across court
2. Pivot on back foot
3. Step across on front foot
4. Step back to T

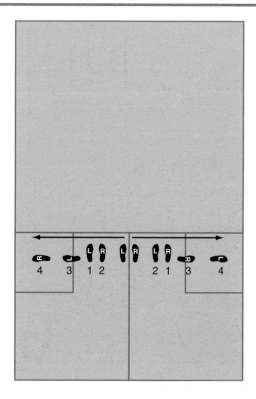

If the ball comes quickly around the service box on your forehand side, it is more efficient to use dynamic midcourt movement. In this situation, often traditional movement will leave you rushed and too close to the ball. After your split step on the T, take a quick shuffle or side step and then reach across with your back foot (figure 2.7). Prepare the racket early, use a short backswing, and turn your shoulders toward the side wall. Once you hit the ball, push directly to the T off your back foot.

Figure 2.7 | Dynamic Midcourt Movement

1. Sidestep across court
2. Step toward side wall with back foot
3. Turn shoulders to side wall before striking ball
4. Step back to T

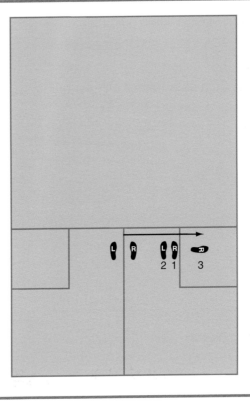

Misstep
You have too much court to cover to retrieve the ball.

Correction
Move back to the T after your shot.

BACKCOURT MOVEMENT

Movement to the back of the court is the most difficult. It is easy to end up off balance or too close to the ball to make a good swing. Always try to use traditional movement on the backhand side in the backcourt, but as with the midcourt movement, you should use both traditional and dynamic movement on the forehand side depending on the situation. If the ball is coming off the back wall and you have time to get into position and transfer your weight to your front foot as you strike the ball, you should use traditional movement. If you are stepping back to the ball before the ball reaches the back wall, it is best to use dynamic movement.

When using traditional backcourt movement, after your split step, use a J-shaped movement and shuffling or sidestepping motion. Move back and then across to the ball (figure 2.8). Ideally, you'll want to get into a midstance—feet about shoulder-width apart and almost parallel to the side wall. Often it works best to position your feet quickly and then make some final small shuffles to adjust to the correct position for hitting the ball. Sometimes, however, you won't have time to get into the midstance; it will then be necessary to pivot on the back foot and step across to the ball on the front foot as you would do with traditional movement in the front- and midcourt. After hitting out of the back corner, step toward the half-court line if you hit a straight drive (to give your opponent a direct line to the ball); otherwise, you can move straight to the T.

Figure 2.8   Traditional Backcourt Movement

1. Sidestep when possible
2. Move back and then across
3. Use midstance
4. Step back toward half-court line

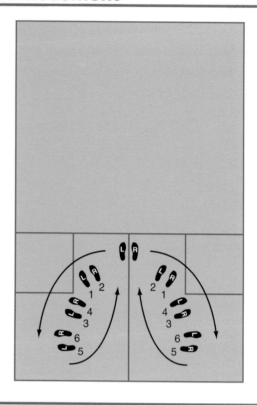

During a rally you may find that you're unable to recover to the T before your opponent hits a shot and that you have more of the court to cover. In this case, take large steps to cover the court quickly and stretch with your last step so that you can reach out farther with the racket face and get lower to the ball. Stretching and bending are the keys to the amazing retrievals made by top players. Remember that when you're out of position, desperate measures are often required to get the ball back into play. It may sometimes be necessary to improvise your footwork or make the wrong movement to get the ball back. Sidestepping to the back corner, for example, isn't practical if you have to cover much of the court in a short time.

Dynamic backcourt movement is similar to dynamic midcourt movement. Use this movement only on the forehand side. Ideally, use it when you are stepping back to hit a shot before the ball reaches the back wall. After your split step, turn slightly toward the back and take a side step toward the back of the service box. Reach out toward the ball with a large stride with your back foot (figure 2.9). Prepare the racket early with a backswing that is shorter than normal. Turn your shoulders toward the side wall before striking the ball. After hitting the ball, push back to the middle off your back foot. Be sure to give your opponent a direct path to the ball. Even if you hit a straight drive, you likely will still need to push back toward the half-court line to allow your opponent to move in front of you to the ball.

Figure 2.9   Dynamic Backcourt Movement

1. Turn and sidestep toward back of service box
2. Take large step to ball with back foot
3. Turn shoulders to side wall before striking ball
4. Step back toward half-court line

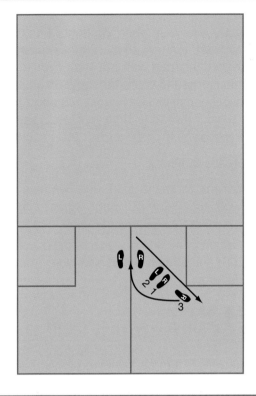

COURT MOVEMENT DRILLS

The best drills for court movement are ghosting exercises in which you move from the T to the corners or sides of the court, play an imaginary (shadow) stroke, and then move back to the T.

When ghosting, use the correct footwork and play a proper stroke. Prepare and swing as if you were going to hit the ball. Move quickly without compromising the quality of your movement and swing.

Court Movement Drill 1. *Front Corners*

Start on the T. Run forward in a J shape to a front corner. Play an imaginary straight drive and then backpedal to the T. Be sure to move back behind the short line before moving forward to repeat the drill to the other front corner. Use figure 2.4 (page 20) as a guide to your footwork. See how long it takes you to do 30 ghosts, 15 to each corner.

To Increase Difficulty

- On the forehand side, use dynamic footwork (see figure 2.5, page 21), or alternate between traditional and dynamic footwork.

To Decrease Difficulty

- Don't time yourself. Instead, concentrate on the quality of your movement.

Success Check

- Use a J-shaped movement.
- Prepare the racket early.
- Backpedal to the T.

Score Your Success

30 ghosts in less than 2 1/2 minutes = 10 points

30 ghosts in 2 1/2 to 3 minutes = 5 points

30 ghosts in more than 3 minutes = 1 point

Your score ___

Court Movement Drill 2. *Side to Side*

Start on the T. Sidestep across, turn, and play an imaginary shot with your forehand. Push back off your front foot toward the T, making sure you turn toward the front wall, not away from it. Then sidestep across the court, turn, and hit an imaginary backhand shot. Use figure 2.6 (page 22) as a guide to your footwork. Time yourself to see how long it takes you to do 50 ghosts, 25 to each side.

To Increase Difficulty

- On the forehand side, use dynamic footwork (see figure 2.7, page 23), or alternate between traditional and dynamic footwork.
- Use only one side step across the court; then turn and stretch across with your front foot as far as possible.

To Decrease Difficulty

- Don't time yourself. Instead, concentrate on the quality of your movement.

Success Check

- Sidestep across the court.
- Pivot on your back foot.
- Step across on your front foot.

Score Your Success

50 ghosts in less than 2 minutes = 10 points

50 ghosts in 2 to 2 1/2 minutes = 5 points

50 ghosts in more than 2 1/2 minutes =1 point

Your score ___

Court Movement Drill 3. *Back Corners*

Start on the T. Turn and sidestep toward a back corner; then take a small step across with your front foot and play an imaginary straight drive. Push off your front foot and sidestep back through the T toward the other back corner. Use figure 2.8 (page 24) as a guide to your footwork. Time yourself to see how long it takes to do 30 ghosts, 15 to each side.

To Increase Difficulty

- On the forehand side, use dynamic footwork (see figure 2.9, page 25), or alternate between traditional and dynamic footwork.

To Decrease Difficulty

- Don't time yourself. Instead, concentrate on the quality of your movement.

Success Check

- Use side steps.
- Prepare the racket early.
- Move to and from the T.

Score Your Success

30 ghosts in less than 2 minutes = 10 points

30 ghosts in 2 to 2 1/2 minutes = 5 points

30 ghosts in more than 2 1/2 minutes = 1 point

Your score ___

Court Movement Drill 4. *Star Drill*

This drill combines the first three drills. Move from the T to the front corners and play imaginary shots. Move to the sides, play imaginary shots, and then move to the back corners and play imaginary shots. Try to make your movements through the T as smooth as possible. Don't stop at the T, but move in one continuous motion from one shot to the next. Playing imaginary shots at each of the six points (figure 2.10) is one star. Try to complete five stars as quickly as possible.

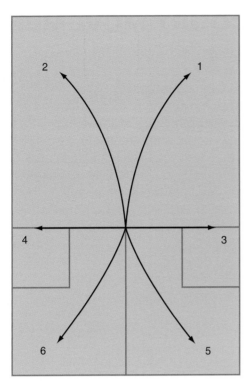

Figure 2.10 Star drill.

To Increase Difficulty

- On the forehand side, use dynamic footwork.

To Decrease Difficulty

- Don't time yourself. Instead, concentrate on the quality of your movement.

Success Check

- Move smoothly through the T.
- Use the correct movements.
- Use a proper swing.

Score Your Success

Five stars in under 1 1/2 minutes = 10 points

Five stars in 1 1/2 to 2 minutes = 5 points

Five stars in more than 2 minutes = 1 point

Your score ___

Court Movement Drill 5. *Random Ghosts*

Number the four corners and two sides of the court from 1 to 6. Have a partner stand against the front wall and randomly call out numbers 1 through 6. You must move from the T to the corresponding area, play an imaginary shot, and return to the T. Your partner calls out the next number just as you return to the T so that you must move to the next position with little hesitation. It can be difficult to remember the corresponding areas while doing this drill, but this is beneficial because you must move while thinking about something else. Therefore, your partner should make you think for yourself by refraining from pointing to the area to which you should be moving. Complete 30 ghost shots as quickly as possible.

To Increase Difficulty

- Have your partner call out either "traditional" or "dynamic" when sending you to the forehand side.

To Decrease Difficulty

- Don't time yourself. Instead, concentrate on the quality of your movement.

Success Check

- Move through the T.
- Split step every time you return to the T.
- Use a proper swing.

Score Your Success

30 imaginary shots in less than 2 minutes = 10 points

30 imaginary shots in 2 to 2 1/2 minutes = 5 points

30 imaginary shots in more than 2 1/2 minutes = 1 point

Your score ___

SUCCESS SUMMARY OF COURT MOVEMENT

You might be fit and have good strokes, but if you don't move efficiently around the court, your opponent can easily and repeatedly catch you off guard. Good court movement consists of allowing yourself enough room to hit the ball, moving smoothly to and from the center of the court, and remaining balanced and ready by staying on the balls of your feet and using the correct stance for a given shot. The ghosting drills in this step will be helpful for both your court movement and fitness, but only if you concentrate on using proper footwork and stroke execution. Have a partner monitor your court movement skills using the key points highlighted in figures 2.4 through 2.9.

Before moving on to step 3, Moving and Hitting in the Frontcourt, evaluate how you did on the drills in this step. Tally your scores to determine how well you have mastered correct court movement. If you scored 40 points or more, you are ready to move on to step 3. If you did not score at least 40 points, practice the drills again until you raise your scores before moving on to step 3.

Court Movement Drills

1. Front Corners	___ out of 10
2. Side to Side	___ out of 10
3. Back Corners	___ out of 10
4. Star Drill	___ out of 10
5. Random Ghosts	___ out of 10
Total	___ *out of 50*

Now that you understand court movement, it is time to start putting together the movement with the hitting that you learned in step 1. Step 3 will teach you how best to combine your court movement and your basic swing in the front of the court. You will learn to move forward and hit the ball both straight and crosscourt into the back corners.

Moving and Hitting in the Frontcourt

Top-level players move and hit so well at the front of the court that they can gain a decisive advantage from an opponent's slightly inaccurate shot to the frontcourt. They can pounce quickly onto any shot that is not hit just above the tin or close to the side wall and dispatch the ball deep into the back corners, forcing their opponents to scramble quickly back to stay in the rally.

Now that you've learned the basic swing and correct court movement, it's time to start putting the two together. When moving and hitting at the front of the court, you should be patient and move smoothly. Most beginners rush around the court and often find themselves too close to the ball and off balance when trying to make their shots. One reason that players rush so much is that they don't realize how much time they have.

Because they haven't yet developed an understanding of good basic strategy, low-level players play the majority of their shots low on the front wall into the frontcourt area. If you can't move and hit well from the front of the court, you'll find yourself giving up easy points against these players. Learning some basic ideas about moving and hitting in the frontcourt will enable you to elevate your game. You'll force your opponents to hit lower on the front wall, which will cause them to make more errors. To pressure you, they'll have to hit shots deeper in the court.

MOVING IN THE FRONTCOURT

After every shot, try to move to the middle of the court (the T), because from there you'll be able to cover all four corners. If, after hitting, you wait for your opponent to hit before moving, you'll occasionally be lucky and have the ball returned to you. But more often than not you'll find yourself working twice as hard as you should, chasing the ball across the court.

Try to get to the T just before your opponent hits the ball, but don't move so fast that you can't concentrate on the ball and stay balanced, ready to change direction quickly. Balance is everything; with it you're able to retrieve many more of your opponent's shots because you're always ready to move quickly in any direction.

Don't forget when you get to the T and your opponent is just about to strike the ball to do a split step, which will put you on the balls of your feet. Hold your racket slightly to your side with the racket face up. Letting the racket face fall to your feet will cause you to take more time preparing for your shot, which often leads to rushed strokes.

Don't stand with your body facing straight at the front wall. Instead, turn your body 45 degrees so that it's facing the front corner of the side from which your opponent is hitting (figure 3.1). From this position you'll be able to turn easily and watch the ball, even if it's right in the back corner. Always watch the ball, especially while your opponent is hitting it. It's easy to turn away from the ball a fraction of a second too soon and end up moving the wrong way.

Figure 3.1   Ready Position at the T

1. Split step
2. On balls of feet
3. Racket to side, racket face up
4. Body turned 45 degrees and facing front corner

Misstep
You are late reacting to your opponent's shot and are unable to hit the ball.

Correction
Keep your eye on the ball. Don't turn away from your opponent until he has hit a shot.

When moving to the ball in the front corners, think about moving to a position to the side of the ball. Don't run straight at the ball because you'll end up too close to the ball to make a smooth swing. Instead, move in a slight J shape, and begin to turn your front shoulder. Pivot on your back foot before making your last step with your front foot into the shot. This will help you get into a sideways position to strike the ball (figure 3.2). Try not to rush; remember that good timing will increase your power and control. Keep your movement and swing as effortless as possible.

Figure 3.2   Move to a position beside the ball before striking it.

Misstep
You are too close to the ball to use a full swing.

Correction
Usually, this error is caused by running straight at the ball instead of using a slight J shape when using traditional movement. In addition to using the J shape, keep your movement smooth and controlled.

On the forehand side, it can be helpful to use dynamic movement to the front of the court if you are under a lot of pressure. Using dynamic movement helps you to stretch farther with your racket. This will enable you to reach shots that you might otherwise not be able to get to with traditional movement.

HITTING IN THE FRONTCOURT WITH TRADITIONAL MOVEMENT

You should use traditional movement as much as possible in the frontcourt because this will put you in the best position for a variety of shots. Your movement and preparation should be the same regardless of whether you are hitting the ball straight or crosscourt. At first, focus on hitting shots to the back corners. Steps 7, 8, and 9 cover hitting shots to the front of the court.

Hitting Straight Shots

Although players typically find it easier to hit crosscourt rather than straight, you will be a far stronger player if you can hit the majority of your shots from the frontcourt straight down the side wall. Your opponent will have a tougher time dealing with shots that are tight to the side wall and end up in the back corners than she will dealing with crosscourt shots that can be hit in the middle of the court.

Hit your straight shots with good depth, deep enough to take your opponent into the back corners. Try to keep your drives tight to the side wall with the first bounce just beyond the service box so that the second bounce is close to the back wall (figure 3.3).

Remember to prepare the racket early, well before you make the last step into the shot (figures 3.4a and 3.5a). Time your movement to the ball so that your final step is with your front foot just before you begin your swing. Strike the ball level with your front foot (figures 3.4b and 3.5b).

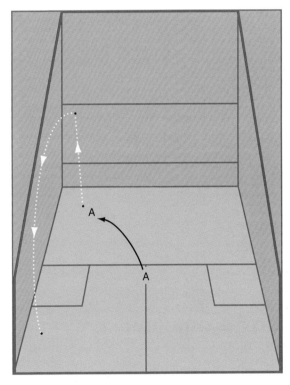

Figure 3.3 Player movement and ball path for a straight drive.

While striking the ball, keep your back foot still; don't let it slide or lift completely off the floor. This will help keep your body still and help you maintain control of the shot. After you've followed through with the shot, push back off your front foot and backpedal toward the T (figures 3.4c and 3.5c).

Figure 3.4   Hitting Forehand Straight Shots

PREPARATION

1. Prepare racket early
2. Cock wrist
3. Bend elbow
4. Make final step with front foot

a

EXECUTION

1. Hit ball level with front foot
2. Keep back foot still
3. Get down low to ball
4. Keep racket face open

b

FOLLOW-THROUGH

1. Bring racket up
2. Push back off front foot
3. Backpedal to T
4. Turn and watch ball

c

| Figure 3.5 | Hitting Backhand Straight Shots |

PREPARATION

1. Prepare racket early
2. Keep racket face close to back of neck
3. Cock wrist
4. Keep elbow in close to body
5. Point elbow downward
6. Make final step with front foot

a

EXECUTION

1. Hit ball level with front foot
2. Keep back foot still
3. Get down low to ball
4. Keep wrist firm and still cocked

b

FOLLOW-THROUGH

1. Bring racket face up
2. Bend elbow
3. Push back off front foot
4. Backpedal to T
5. Turn and watch ball

c

Hitting Crosscourt Shots

If you try to hit everything straight from the front, you will become too predictable. You need to hit some crosscourt shots to mix up your game. Hit crosscourt shots with good depth and width so that your opponent must move back to retrieve the ball. The shot should hit the side wall toward the back of the service box. The ball should then bounce on the floor close to the back wall (figure 3.6). Don't aim crosscourt shots straight at the back corner. The ball will pass through the middle of the court where your opponent can cut it off before it reaches the back of the court.

Prepare for the crosscourt in the same way as you would for a straight drive, and make the final step with your front foot just before you begin your swing. However, for a crosscourt shot, you should strike the ball slightly farther forward from your front foot (figures 3.7 and 3.8). Again, it is important to keep your back foot still as you strike the ball and to push off your front foot back toward the T.

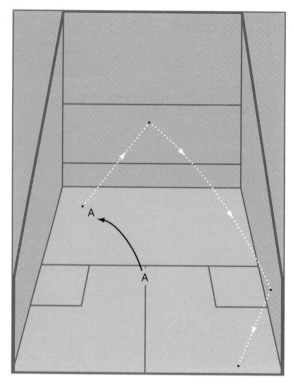

Figure 3.6 Player movement and ball path for a crosscourt drive.

| **Figure 3.7** | **Hitting Forehand Crosscourt Shots** |

1. Hit ball just forward from front foot
2. Make sure shot has plenty of width
3. Recover to T quickly and smoothly

Figure 3.8 Hitting Backhand Crosscourt Shots

1. Hit ball just forward from front foot
2. Make sure shot has plenty of width
3. Recover to T quickly and smoothly

Misstep
Your opponent cuts off your shots.

Correction
Hit your shot with more height and more width to make it difficult for your opponent to volley your shot.

HITTING IN THE FRONTCOURT WITH DYNAMIC MOVEMENT

Sometimes, if you are under significant pressure, you can reach farther and therefore retrieve more shots in the frontcourt if you use dynamic movement rather than traditional movement. It is always best to use traditional movement and lead with your front foot into the shot if you have the time to do so because this makes it easier to turn your shoulders and allows you to get more power in your shots. On the forehand side, if you reach forward with your back foot toward the ball, you can stretch farther into the front corner. It is not recommended to reach forward with your back foot on the backhand side unless you have no choice. Not only is it much harder to hit a backhand off the back foot, but also it will actual impede rather than improve your reach into the front of the court.

When using dynamic movement, after your split step on the T, move straight toward the ball. Do this only if you are under pressure and do not have time to use the J-shaped movement. Prepare your racket early, but use a slightly shorter backswing (figure 3.9a). Time your movement so that you take a large final step to the ball with your back foot. Turn your shoulders so that they face the side wall. If possible, try to hit the ball to the side of your front foot. When under pressure, often you will be forced to hit the ball slightly farther forward from your front foot (figure 3.9b). Try to keep your feet still as you strike the ball. If hitting a straight drive, use a short, punchy swing. If hitting a crosscourt shot, make sure you hit either high on the front wall or with good width to get the ball past your opponent. After your swing, push off your back (leading) foot and backpedal to the T (figure 3.9c).

Figure 3.9   Hitting Forehand Shots With Dynamic Movement

PREPARATION

1. Move straight at ball
2. Use shorter backswing
2. Make final step with back foot

a

EXECUTION

1. Use short, punchy swing
2. Keep feet still
3. Get down low to ball

b

FOLLOW-THROUGH

1. Bring racket up
2. Push off leading foot

c

Misstep

You feel rushed when striking the ball.

Correction

Prepare your racket as soon as you see to which side the ball is going. This will give you much more time to position yourself and strike the ball. Use dynamic movement when under pressure on the forehand side.

When you've hit a shot to the backcourt, you should feel confident about covering any shot your opponent hits to the front. If you don't yet have this confidence, you must continue to work hard on moving and hitting in the frontcourt.

Moving and Hitting in the Frontcourt Drill 1.
Drives From the Front Corner

Stand on the T and throw the ball high into the front corner so that it hits the front wall and side wall and then bounces on the floor about 6 feet (1.8 m) from the front (figure 3.10). Run forward and drive the ball into the back corner no farther from the side wall than the width of the service box. Hit 10 forehand drives and 10 backhand drives. Try to hit past the back of the service box.

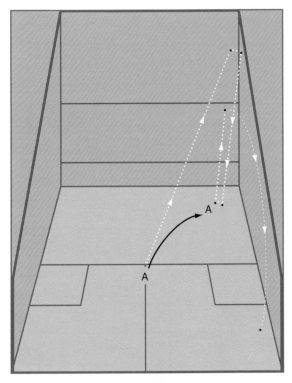

Figure 3.10 Drives from the front corner.

To Increase Difficulty

- Vary the pace of your drives.
- Throw the ball lower on the front wall.
- Aim at a target in the back corner.
- On the forehand side, use dynamic movement.

To Decrease Difficulty

- Throw the ball higher on the front wall.
- Move a little closer to the front wall before throwing the ball.

Success Check

- Hit the ball to the side of your front foot.
- Aim high on the front wall for depth.
- Keep your back foot still as you swing.

Score Your Success

8 to 10 forehand drives that hit past the back of the service box = 5 points

6 or 7 forehand drives that hit past the back of the service box = 3 points

4 or 5 forehand drives that hit past the back of the service box = 1 point

8 to 10 backhand drives that hit past the back of the service box = 5 points

6 or 7 backhand drives that hit past the back of the service box = 3 points

4 or 5 backhand drives that hit past the back of the service box = 1 point

Your score ___

Moving and Hitting in the Frontcourt Drill 2.
Crosscourt Shots From the Front Corner

This drill is the same as the first except that instead of hitting straight drives, you play a crosscourt drive into the opposite back corner (figure 3.11). The ball should hit the opposite side wall behind the short line and then bounce on the floor between the back of the service box and the back wall. Hit 10 forehand crosscourt shots and 10 backhand crosscourt shots. Try to hit the side wall behind the short line.

To Increase Difficulty

- Throw the ball lower on the front wall.
- Aim at a target in the back corner.
- On the forehand side, use dynamic movement.

To Decrease Difficulty

- Throw the ball higher on the front wall.

Success Check

- Hit the ball slightly forward from your front foot.
- Keep your back foot still as you swing.
- Push off your front foot after the follow-through.

Score Your Success

8 to 10 forehand crosscourt shots that hit the side wall behind the short line = 5 points

6 or 7 forehand crosscourt shots that hit the side wall behind the short line = 3 points

4 or 5 forehand crosscourt shots that hit the side wall behind the short line = 1 point

8 to 10 backhand crosscourt shots that hit the side wall behind the short line = 5 points

6 or 7 backhand crosscourt shots that hit the side wall behind the short line = 3 points

4 or 5 backhand crosscourt shots that hit the side wall behind the short line = 1 point

Your score ___

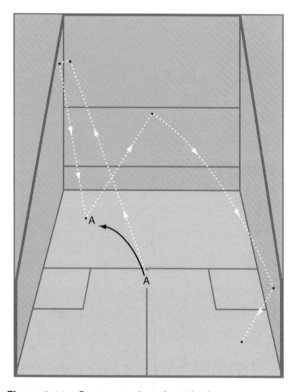

Figure 3.11   Crosscourt shots from the front corner.

Moving and Hitting in the Frontcourt Drill 3.
Straight Drives From a Partner's Feed

Have a partner stand in the back corner and feed a soft shot that hits the front wall about 1 to 2 feet (0.3 to 0.6 m) above the tin (figure 3.12). Move forward from the T and hit a straight drive. If possible, your partner should keep the exercise going without stopping between shots. Try to make your drives bounce behind the back of the service box and no farther from the side wall than the width of the service box. Hit 10 forehand straight drives and 10 backhand straight drives. Try to hit the ball so it bounces behind the back of the service box.

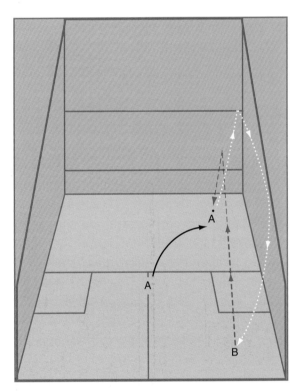

Figure 3.12 Straight drives from a partner's feed.

To Increase Difficulty

- Set a target in the back corner.
- Have your partner stand farther forward and volley your shots.
- On the forehand side, alternate between traditional and dynamic movements.

To Decrease Difficulty

- Have your partner stop after each shot so that you have time to prepare for the next one.

Success Check

- Step across with your front foot.
- Transfer your weight to the front foot as you hit.
- Hit the ball between your body and the side wall.

Score Your Success

8 to 10 forehand straight drives that bounce behind the back of the service box = 5 points

6 or 7 forehand straight drives that bounce behind the back of the service box = 3 points

4 or 5 forehand straight drives that bounce behind the back of the service box = 1 point

8 to 10 backhand straight drives that bounce behind the back of the service box = 5 points

6 or 7 backhand straight drives that bounce behind the back of the service box = 3 points

4 or 5 backhand straight drives that bounce behind the back of the service box = 1 point

Your score ___

Moving and Hitting in the Frontcourt Drill 4.
Crosscourt Drives From a Partner's Feed

Have a partner stand in the back corner and hit a shot off the side wall crosscourt to the opposite front corner (figure 3.13). Move forward from the T and hit a crosscourt drive back to your partner. If possible, your partner should keep the exercise going without stopping between shots. Try to make your crosscourt drives hit the side wall behind the short line and then bounce on the floor between the back of the service box and the back wall. Hit 10 forehand crosscourt drives and 10 backhand crosscourt drives. Try to hit the side wall behind the short line with each crosscourt drive.

To Increase Difficulty

- Set a target in the back corner.
- Have your partner stand farther forward and volley your shots.
- On the forehand side, alternate between traditional and dynamic movements.

To Decrease Difficulty

- Have your partner stop after each shot so that you have time to prepare for the next one.

Success Check

- Hit the ball slightly forward from your front foot.
- Keep your back foot still as you swing.
- Push off your front foot after the follow-through.

Score Your Success

8 to 10 forehand crosscourt drives that hit the side wall behind the short line = 5 points

6 or 7 forehand crosscourt drives that hit the side wall behind the short line = 3 points

4 or 5 forehand crosscourt drives that hit the side wall behind the short line = 1 point

8 to 10 backhand crosscourt drives that hit the side wall behind the short line = 5 points

6 or 7 backhand crosscourt drives that hit the side wall behind the short line = 3 points

4 or 5 backhand crosscourt drives that hit the side wall behind the short line = 1 point

Your score ___

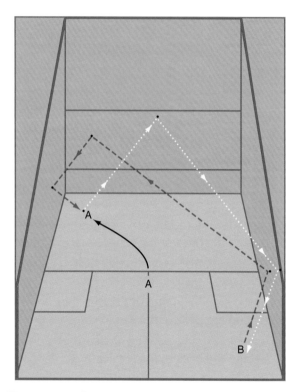

Figure 3.13   Crosscourt drives from a partner's feed.

Moving and Hitting in the Frontcourt Drill 5.
Alternate Drives From a Partner's Feed

This is a combination of the last two drills. Have a partner stand in the back corner and feed a soft shot that hits the front wall about 1 to 2 feet (0.3 to 0.6 m) above the tin. Move forward from the T and hit a straight drive back to your partner. Your partner then hits a shot off the side wall crosscourt to the opposite front corner. Move forward from the T and hit a crosscourt drive back to your partner. If possible, your partner should keep the exercise going without stopping between shots as you alternate between straight and crosscourt drives. Time how long you can keep the drill going without stopping or missing a shot.

To Increase Difficulty

- Have your partner stand farther forward and volley your shots.
- Have your partner mix up the feeds instead of alternating.
- On the forehand side, alternate between traditional and dynamic movements.

To Decrease Difficulty

- Have your partner stop after each shot so that you have time to prepare for the next one.

Success Check

- Turn and watch as your partner strikes the ball.
- Step forward with your front foot.
- Move back to the T after hitting your drive.

Score Your Success

Keep the drill going continuously (forehand straight, backhand crosscourt) for more than 3 minutes = 5 points

Keep the drill going continuously (forehand straight, backhand crosscourt) for 2 to 3 minutes = 3 points

Keep the drill going continuously (forehand straight, backhand crosscourt) for less than 2 minutes = 1 point

Keep the drill going continuously (backhand straight, forehand crosscourt) for more than 3 minutes = 5 points

Keep the drill going continuously (backhand straight, forehand crosscourt) for 2 to 3 minutes = 3 points

Keep the drill going continuously (backhand straight, forehand crosscourt) for less than 2 minutes = 1 point

Your score ___

Moving and Hitting in the Frontcourt Drill 6.
Drives on the Run

Have a partner stand in the back corner and feed short shots to the front of the court (figure 3.14). Hit a straight drive to the back corner, turn and run across to touch the opposite side wall, and return to the middle of the court to get ready for the next shot. Make sure that you turn toward, not away from, the front wall after striking the ball and after touching the side wall. Also, don't hesitate when touching the side wall. Return to the T quickly to give yourself plenty of time for the next shot. Your drive should bounce past the back of the service box and no farther than the width of the service box from the side wall. Hit 10 forehand drives and 10 backhand drives. Try to hit each drive past the back of the service box.

To Increase Difficulty

- Have your partner feed faster and lower so that you must move faster and stretch more for each shot.
- Instead of touching the side wall, turn and play an imaginary shot near the back of the opposite service box.
- Instead of touching the side wall, run backward and touch the back wall between shots.
- On the forehand side, alternate between traditional and dynamic movements.

To Decrease Difficulty

- Have your partner wait longer before feeding the ball so you have plenty of time to move back to the T.
- Have your partner feed the ball higher on the front wall.

Success Check

- Wait on the T while your partner feeds the ball.
- Keep your movement as smooth as possible.
- Push off your front foot after the follow-through.

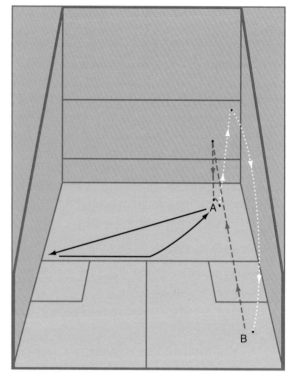

Figure 3.14 Drives on the run.

Score Your Success

10 consecutive forehand drives past the back of the service box = 5 points

7 to 9 consecutive forehand drives past the back of the service box = 3 points

4 to 6 consecutive forehand drives past the back of the service box = 1 point

10 consecutive backhand drives past the back of the service box = 5 points

7 to 9 consecutive backhand drives past the back of the service box = 3 points

4 to 6 consecutive backhand drives past the back of the service box = 1 point

Your score ___

Moving and Hitting in the Frontcourt Drill 7.
Pressure Drives

Stand on the T and have a partner stand in the service box and feed a reverse angle (a shot that hits the opposite side wall before it hits the front wall). The feed should hit the floor after hitting the front wall and then bounce up off the side wall (figure 3.15). Run forward to hit a hard straight drive, which the feeder can catch, and then run backward to the T to be ready for the next feed. Try to hit the ball no farther from the side wall than the width of the service box. Hit 10 forehand drives and 10 backhand drives. Try to hit each drive above the tin.

To Increase Difficulty

- Have your partner hit low, hard reverse angles.
- On the forehand side, alternate between traditional and dynamic movements.

To Decrease Difficulty

- Have your partner hit reverse angles high on the front wall.

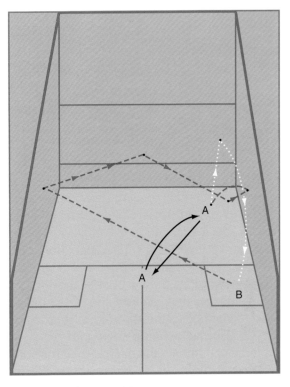

Figure 3.15 Pressure drives.

Success Check

- Return to the T between shots.
- Time your movement so that your last step is just before you swing.
- Keep your body still as you swing.

Score Your Success

8 to 10 forehand drives above the tin = 5 points

6 or 7 forehand drives above the tin = 3 points

4 or 5 forehand drives above the tin = 1 point

8 to 10 backhand drives above the tin = 5 points

6 or 7 backhand drives above the tin = 3 points

4 or 5 backhand drives above the tin = 1 point

Your score ____

Moving and Hitting in the Frontcourt Drill 8.
Backcourt Versus Frontcourt

This is a conditioned, or modified, game in which you must hit every shot behind the short line, and your opponent must hit every shot in front of the short line. You serve at the beginning of each point. Use point-per-rally scoring to 11 points. Play three games.

To Increase Difficulty

- Hit everything straight and behind the short line.

To Decrease Difficulty

- Require your opponent to hit everything straight and in front of the short line.
- Require your opponent to hit shots only off the side wall.

Success Check

- Always watch the ball.
- Move back to the T after each shot.
- Hit high on the front wall when under pressure.

Score Your Success

Win two out of three games against your opponent = 5 points

Win one out of three games against your opponent = 3 points

Your score ___

Moving and Hitting in the Frontcourt Drill 9.
Two-Ball Feeds

This drill requires two feeders, each with a ball, one on the forehand and one on the backhand. The feeders alternate feeding short shots to you. You move from side to side, hitting straight drives back to the feeders (figure 3.16). The feeders should strike their balls in turn, just after you've turned from hitting the last drive. Make sure that you turn toward the front wall when moving from side to side and that you turn and watch the ball as the feeder begins the shot. Staring at the front wall will give you less time to set up for your shot and force you to rush too much. As with all drills involving straight drives, try to make the ball bounce behind the back of the service box and no farther from the side wall than the width of the service box. Time how long you can keep the drill going without missing a shot.

To Increase Difficulty

- Have the feeders feed lower and faster.
- Vary the pace of your drives.
- Set targets in the back corners.

To Decrease Difficulty

- Have the feeders feed higher on the front wall.
- Have the feeders wait until you are on the T before feeding the ball.

Success Check

- Turn toward the front wall after your shot.
- Wait on the T for the feeder to feed the ball.
- Try to stay relaxed as you move.

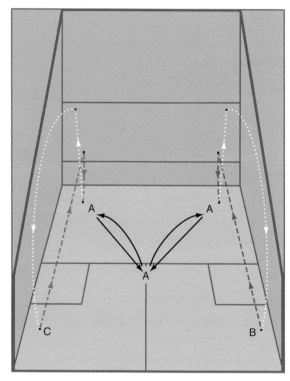

Figure 3.16 Two-ball feeds.

Score Your Success

Keep the drill going continuously for more than 5 minutes = 10 points

Keep the drill going continuously for 4 to 5 minutes = 5 points

Keep the drill going continuously for less than 4 minutes = 1 points

Your score ___

Moving and Hitting in the Frontcourt Drill 10.
Drives Off Short Crosscourt Shots

Player A stands in the back corner and hits a shot that rebounds off the side wall to the front wall (figure 3.17). Player B stands in the opposite front corner and hits a soft shot across the court into the opposite front corner. You (player C) have to run forward from the T, hit a straight drive back to player A, and then backpedal to the T. Hit the drive past the back of the service box and no farther from the side wall than the width of the service box. Rather than stopping after each drive, player A should keep the drill going by hitting off your drive. Hit 10 forehand drives and 10 backhand drives. Try to hit each drive so it hits past the back of the service box.

To Increase Difficulty

- Have player B hit lower on the front wall.
- Set a target area in the back corner.

To Decrease Difficulty

- Have player B hit higher crosscourt drops.
- Have player A stop before hitting to make sure you have time to recover to the T.

Success Check

- Make a large last step to the ball.
- Run backward to the T.
- Keep your eye on the ball.

Score Your Success

8 to 10 forehand drives past the back of the service box = 5 points

6 or 7 forehand drives past the back of the service box = 3 points

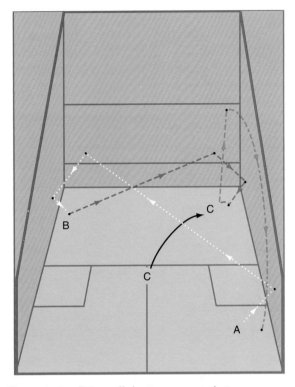

Figure 3.17 Drives off short crosscourt shots.

4 or 5 forehand drives past the back of the service box = 1 point

8 to 10 backhand drives past the back of the service box = 5 points

6 or 7 backhand drives past the back of the service box = 3 points

4 or 5 backhand drives past the back of the service box = 1 point

Your score ___

Moving and Hitting in the Frontcourt Drill 11.
Alternating Drives

This is similar to drill 10 except that player B hits straight instead of crosscourt (figure 3.18). You must move forward and hit a straight drive, alternating between forehand and backhand. Before moving toward the ball, allow player B to step back toward the middle of the court to clear a path for you. Player A moves from side to side in the backcourt, keeping the drill going continuously. See how many consecutive drives you can hit without letting the ball bounce twice.

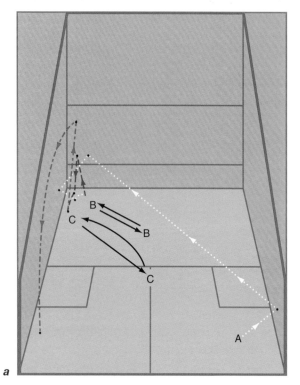 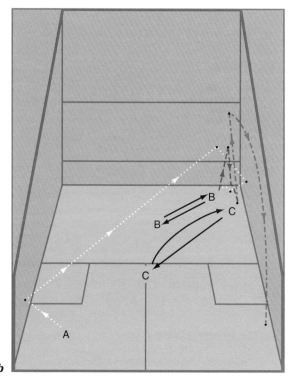

Figure 3.18 Alternating drives: *(a)* player A begins on the right side of the court; *(b)* player A moves to the left side of the court to keep the drill going.

To Increase Difficulty

- Allow player B to hit either straight or crosscourt.
- Allow player B any choice of shot at the front, including hitting off the side wall to the front wall.

To Decrease Difficulty

- Have player B hit higher on the front wall to give you more time to reach the shot.

Success Check

- Prepare your racket early.
- Bend low to the ball.
- Watch the ball as you backpedal to the T.

Score Your Success

20 or more consecutive straight drives without letting the ball bounce twice = 10 points

15 to 19 consecutive straight drives without letting the ball bounce twice = 5 points

14 or fewer consecutive straight drives without letting the ball bounce twice = 1 point

Your score ___

SUCCESS SUMMARY OF MOVING AND HITTING IN THE FRONTCOURT

The four keys to success when hitting the ball in the frontcourt are being ready at the T, maintaining balance, keeping your eye on the ball, and using J-shaped movements. Be sure to hit with good depth and good width to drive your opponent into the back corners. Don't allow your shots to be cut off in midcourt. Remember to backpedal quickly but smoothly to the T after making your shot. On the forehand side, use dynamic movement if you are under pressure and quickly need to stretch for the ball. Have your coach critique your movement and hitting in the frontcourt using figures 3.4, 3.5, 3.7, 3.8, and 3.9.

Before moving on to step 4, Moving and Hitting in the Backcourt, evaluate how you did on the drills in this step. Tally your scores to determine how well you have mastered correct frontcourt movement and hitting. If you scored 85 points or more, you are ready to move on to step 4. If you did not score at least 85 points, practice the drills again until you raise your scores before moving on to step 4.

Moving and Hitting in the Frontcourt Drills

1. Drives From the Front Corner	___ out of 10
2. Crosscourt Shots From the Front Corner	___ out of 10
3. Straight Drives From a Partner's Feed	___ out of 10
4. Crosscourt Drives From a Partner's Feed	___ out of 10
5. Alternate Drives From a Partner's Feed	___ out of 10
6. Drives on the Run	___ out of 10
7. Pressure Drives	___ out of 10
8. Backcourt Versus Frontcourt	___ out of 5
9. Two-Ball Feeds	___ out of 10
10. Drives Off Short Crosscourt Shots	___ out of 10
11. Alternating Drives	___ out of 10
Total	___ **out of 105**

Now that you have mastered moving and hitting in the frontcourt, it is time to move to the back area. Step 4 will help you combine your basic forehand and backhand swings from step 1 with your court movement from step 2 to move and hit correctly in the backcourt.

Moving and Hitting in the Backcourt

Most squash coaches advise hitting at least 80 percent of shots to the back corners because hitting out of the backcourt is so difficult. If you can keep your opponent pinned in the backcourt, you'll have easy opportunities to win points at the front of the court. It's difficult to hit out of the back corners because the swing is restricted by both the side wall and the back wall.

Remember that while you're trying to pin your opponent in the backcourt, he is trying to do the same to you. To hit well out of the back corners, you must maintain good movement and position, know when to strike the ball early

and when to wait for it to bounce off the back wall, and have the confidence to bend down and strike the ball close to the floor.

As you play better opponents, you'll find that they will attack you by first driving you deep into the back corners and then by looking for opportunities to make you run from the back of the court to the front corners. If you don't develop good movement and hitting out of the backcourt, you'll find yourself hitting weak shots off your opponent's deep shots, which will give your opponent many easy opportunities to work you hard in the front of the court.

MOVING TO AND FROM THE BACK CORNERS

When moving to the back corners from the T, make sure you don't run straight at the ball. Think about trying to stay to the side of the ball as you move back (figure 4.1). It's much easier to make a large final step toward the ball just before you hit it than to move back quickly to give yourself room to swing. Therefore, your movement in the back corners, like your movement in the front corners, should follow a slightly

curved route toward the corner rather than a straight line.

After hitting a straight drive from the back, move behind your opponent and then up the middle of the court to the T (figure 4.2). However, if you step across and cut off the ball before it reaches the back wall, or if your opponent overhits and the ball rebounds off the back wall back toward the middle of the court,

Figure 4.1 Use a side step to move to a position beside the ball before striking it.

then you may be able to cut straight back to the T without moving behind your opponent. Remember, though, that you must give your opponent freedom to move directly to the ball. So if your opponent is trying to move in front of you to the ball and you're in the way, you're probably making the wrong movement back to the T.

If you're in doubt about which way your opponent is going to move to the ball, it's best just to concentrate on hitting a tight shot, waiting to see which way your opponent moves, and then going the other way back to the T. Don't rush your shot to cut straight to the T. This often leads to a poor shot out from the side wall, which may end up costing you the point. When cutting off the ball, good players often choose to hit a crosscourt shot so they don't risk hitting the ball back to themselves.

a

b

Figure 4.2 *(a)* Move around the back of your opponent *(b)* to return to the T.

FOREHAND SHOTS IN THE BACKCOURT

On the forehand side in the backcourt, it is best to use traditional movement if you are hitting the ball after it hits the floor and then the back wall. Because the ball often comes off the back wall slowly, it is important to get into a position in which you can really turn your body toward the corner to ensure that you are generating plenty of power in the shot from your shoulders. If you are cutting the ball off before it reaches the back wall, it is best to use dynamic movement and step back with your back foot just before you swing.

When hitting a forehand out of the back corner with traditional movement, it's best to use a midstance (figure 4.3a). Turn your body very slightly toward the back corner, but not so far that you to have to flick your wrist to get the ball to go straight down the side wall. Ideally, you'll set up your feet in plenty of time to pause for a second before playing the shot. It is very important to transfer your weight onto your front foot just before you strike the ball to get your momentum into the stroke. Sometimes a small step with the front foot helps with this.

Be sure to keep your racket up high while waiting to play the shot. Make sure you keep your wrist cocked and your elbow slightly bent. Resist the temptation to drop the racket face down and flick the ball. Instead, bend your knees and crouch down. The midstance enables you to bend your knees quite a long way and stay balanced. Leave plenty of room to swing between yourself and the ball, and turn your front shoulder toward the back corner so you can generate power in your shot from the backswing. Stay still while striking the ball and following through, being sure not to move your front foot or your hips. Remember to keep your wrist firm and press through the ball as much as possible (figure 4.3b).

On the follow-through keep your body still and bring your racket face up (figure 4.3c). Once you have completed the shot, push off your front foot back toward the half-court line and then move up to the T. Allow your opponent enough room to move in front of you to the ball.

| Figure 4.3 | Hitting Forehand Drives in the Backcourt, Traditional Movement |

PREPARATION

1. Turn body slightly toward back corner
2. Place feet shoulder-width apart
3. Wait for ball to come back off back wall as far as possible
4. Keep racket up
5. Cock wrist
6. Bend elbow
7. Bend knees

a

(continued)

Figure 4.3 (continued)

b

c

EXECUTION

1. Keep wrist firm
2. Keep racket face open
3. Push up through ball
4. Keep feet still

FOLLOW-THROUGH

1. Keep body still
2. Bring racket face up to front shoulder
3. Push off front foot

Misstep

Your straight drives hit the side wall before they hit the front wall.

Correction

Make sure that you're standing close to the back wall. Wait for the ball to bounce as far off the back wall as possible. Hit the ball out to the side of your front foot.

When hitting a forehand out of the back corner with dynamic movement, after your split step on the T, take side steps in the middle of the court as necessary and then take a large step across with your back foot. Before taking that last step, prepare your racket with a slightly shorter backswing. You must still turn your front shoulder toward the side wall as much as possible (figure 4.4a). If you have enough time to prepare early and get a good shoulder turn, you can attack the shot and drive it hard, either straight or crosscourt. But if you're rushed or are backing up close to the back wall and can't get a good shoulder turn, it's normally best to open the racket face and hit underneath the ball, placing a high, soft shot straight down the side wall (figure 4.4b).

After striking the ball, keep your body still as you follow through (figure 4.4c). Push off your back foot toward the half-court line. You must give your opponent direct access to the ball. If you hit a straight drive and your opponent is moving in front of you, it is important that you push back to the side to allow her through before moving forward to return to the T.

Figure 4.4 **Hitting Forehand Drives in the Backcourt, Dynamic Movement**

PREPARATION

1. Step back to ball with back foot
2. Turn shoulders so they face side wall
3. Use slightly shorter backswing
4. Keep racket up
5. Bend knees

a

EXECUTION

1. Keep wrist firm
2. Keep racket face open
3. Keep feet still

b

FOLLOW-THROUGH

1. Keep body still
2. Bring racket face up
3. Push off back foot

c

BACKHAND SHOTS IN THE BACKCOURT

Whether you are waiting for the ball to come off the back wall or cutting off the ball before it reaches the back wall, on the backhand side it is always best to use traditional movement, stepping across with your front foot. Whenever possible, use the midstance (figure 4.5a). As on the forehand side, turn your body very slightly toward the back corner and set up your feet about a shoulder's width apart in plenty of time to pause for a second before playing the shot. It is very important to transfer your weight onto your front foot just before you strike the ball to get your momentum into the stroke. Sometimes a small step with the front foot helps with this.

Be sure to keep your racket up around the back of your neck. Make sure you keep your wrist cocked and your knuckles facing up. Your elbow should be in close to your body and should

be pointing down toward the floor. Bend your knees and crouch down; do not drop the racket face down and flick the ball. Give yourself plenty of room to swing, and turn your front shoulder toward the back corner so you can generate power in your shot from the backswing. Stay still while striking the ball and following through. Again, be sure not to move your front foot or your hips. Press through the ball with your wrist firm (figure 4.5b).

On the follow-through keep your body still and bring your racket face up above your head (figure 4.5c). Bend your elbow as you follow through so that your racket head still stays fairly close to you at the end of your follow-through. Once you have completed the shot, push off your front foot toward the half-court line and then move up to the T. Allow your opponent enough room to move in front of you to the ball.

Figure 4.5   Hitting Backhand Shots in the Backcourt

PREPARATION

1. Turn body slightly toward back corner
2. Place feet shoulder-width apart
3. Wait for ball to come back off back wall as far as possible
4. Keep racket face close to back of neck
5. Cock wrist
6. Keep elbow in close to body
7. Keep elbow pointing down
8. Bend knees

a

EXECUTION

1. Keep wrist firm
2. Keep racket face open
3. Push up through ball
4. Keep feet still

b

FOLLOW-THROUGH

1. Keep body still
2. Bring racket face up above head
3. Bend elbow
4. Push off front foot

c

If you are hitting the ball before it reaches the back wall, it is unlikely you will have the time to get into the midstance before striking the ball. In this instance turn your body and step across toward the side wall with your front foot (figure 4.6). Your body will be turned so that it is almost completely facing the back wall. It is extremely important to begin preparing the racket for the backswing before you even start to turn your body because you will want to time your step across on the front foot so that you swing immediately after planting the front foot on the floor. The execution and follow-through for the shot are exactly the same as if you were in the midstance.

Figure 4.6 Preparation for a backhand shot when cutting off the ball before it reaches the back wall.

Misstep
Your opponent cuts off your shots.

Correction
Hit with less power so that you can concentrate on accuracy. If your shot isn't bouncing past the back of the service box, think about trying to hit higher on the front wall.

Smoothness in your movement and confidence in the way you strike the ball should be your goals when moving and hitting in the backcourt. If you find yourself stretched and off balance in the back corners, open your racket face and hit a soft shot high onto the front wall to get the necessary width and depth. Trying to hit too hard when off balance normally leads to loss of control. The ball ends up too short and in the middle of the court.

The better your ability to bend low and stay balanced, the easier you'll find it to hit shots straight out of the back corners. Sometimes, however, the ball will be too low to hit straight. In this case turn your front shoulder farther around toward the back wall and boast the ball onto the front wall. A boast is a shot that rebounds off the side wall first before hitting the front wall. The boast is covered in more depth in step 7.

Misstep
You are too close to the ball to use a full swing.

Correction
Be sure that your first movement from the T is almost directly backward rather than across and then back to the corner. Use dynamic movement when cutting off the ball on the forehand side.

Moving and Hitting in the Backcourt Drill 1.
Drives From the Back Corner

Stand in the back corner about 2 feet (0.6 m) from the back wall and 5 feet (1.5 m) from the side wall. Face the side wall with your racket face up. Throw the ball against the side wall so that it bounces about 2 feet (0.6 m) from your front foot. Hit a straight drive to the back corner, keeping the ball no farther from the side wall than the width of the service box (figure 4.7). Hit 10 forehand drives and 10 backhand drives. Try to hit each drive so it bounces beyond the back of the service box.

To Increase Difficulty

• Set a target in the back corner to aim at.
• Throw the ball against the back wall instead of the side wall.
• Hit crosscourt shots at a target in the opposite back corner.

To Decrease Difficulty

• Stand farther forward in the court.

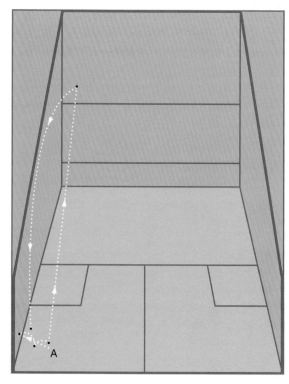

Figure 4.7 Drives from back corner.

Success Check

- Prepare your racket before you throw the ball.
- Use a midstance.
- Keep your feet still as you swing.

Score Your Success

8 to 10 forehand drives that bounce beyond the back of the service box = 5 points

6 or 7 forehand drives that bounce beyond the back of the service box = 3 points

4 or 5 forehand drives that bounce beyond the back of the service box = 1 point

8 to 10 backhand drives that bounce beyond the back of the service box = 5 points

6 or 7 backhand drives that bounce beyond the back of the service box = 3 points

4 or 5 backhand drives that bounce beyond the back of the service box = 1 point

Your score ___

Moving and Hitting in the Backcourt Drill 2.
Continuous Drives

This is similar to drill 1, except this time you try to hit continuous drives, keeping a rally going with yourself as long you can. Try to make all your shots hit the floor and then the back wall, although be prepared to step in early to hit the ball if you think it's going to die before it hits the back wall. Once the ball hits the back wall, wait for it to rebound as far from the back wall as possible before striking it. If you overhit a drive so that it bounces off the back wall before it hits the floor, take much of the pace off your next shot. The momentum of the ball flying off the back wall makes it easy to overhit the second shot as well.

To Increase Difficulty

- Vary the pace of your shots.
- Hit three straight drives and then a cross-court shot.
- Decrease the size of the target area.

To Decrease Difficulty

- Let the ball bounce a second time after it hits the back wall.
- Keep a rally going by hitting softer shots that don't hit the back wall.

Success Check

- Wait for the ball to drop before you strike it.
- Bend your knees.
- Aim high on the front wall.

Score Your Success

10 or more consecutive forehand drives = 5 points

6 to 9 consecutive forehand drives = 3 points

5 or fewer consecutive forehand drives = 1 point

10 or more consecutive backhand drives = 5 points

6 to 9 consecutive backhand drives = 3 points

5 or fewer consecutive backhand drives = 1 point

Your score ___

Moving and Hitting in the Backcourt Drill 3.
Backcourt Drives on the Run

Have a partner stand on the T and feed you a straight drive to the back corner. Hit a straight drive from the back, aiming the ball to hit above the service line and staying within a service-box width of the side wall (figure 4.8). Then turn, move across, and touch the opposite side wall before returning to the back corner to get ready for the next feed. The feeder should try to stop the ball before it passes so that she can quickly feed the next drive. On the forehand side, use traditional movement if you are hitting the ball after it hits the back wall or if you have plenty of time to step forward into your shot. Use dynamic movement if you are cutting off the ball before it hits the back

wall and are reaching across or back for it. Hit as many consecutive forehand drives as you can; then switch to backhand drives.

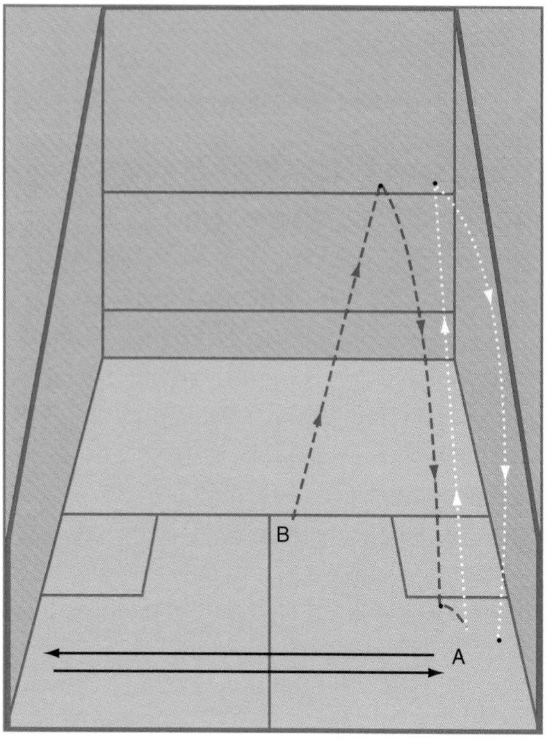

To Increase Difficulty

- Run forward and across, touching the side wall in front of the opposite service box between shots.
- Have your partner feed as quickly as possible.

To Decrease Difficulty

- Have your partner wait for you to get back in position before feeding the ball.

Success Check

- Finish your follow-through before turning to move toward the side wall.
- Turn toward the front wall.
- Give yourself plenty of room to hit.

Score Your Success

20 or more consecutive forehand drives above the service line = 10 points

10 to 19 consecutive forehand drives above the service line = 5 points

9 or fewer consecutive forehand drives above the service line = 1 point

20 or more consecutive backhand drives above the service line = 10 points

10 to 19 consecutive backhand drives above the service line = 5 points

9 or fewer consecutive backhand drives above the service line = 1 point

Your score ___

Figure 4.8   Backcourt drives on the run.

Moving and Hitting in the Backcourt Drill 4.
Backcourt Rallying

With a partner, play a rally in the back corner, hitting only straight drives. Make sure that you circle around each other. That is, after you have struck the ball, move behind your partner to the T (figure 4.9). Avoid becoming stuck in the back corner while your opponent stands in front cutting off all your shots. Be sure your shots are deep into the backcourt and close to the side wall. Make sure that you prepare your racket smoothly, because whipping it back too quickly may endanger your opponent. Time how long you and your partner can rally without a miss while hitting forehands; then switch to backhands.

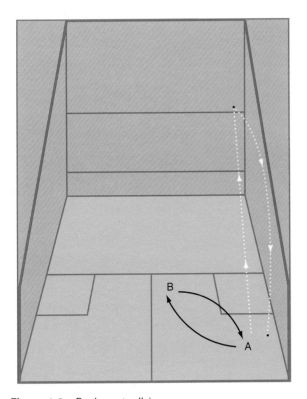

Figure 4.9 Backcourt rallying.

To Increase Difficulty

- Set target areas (e.g., all shots must bounce behind the back of the service box and no farther from the side wall than the width of the service box).
- Play a conditioned, or modified, game. The first person to miss the target area loses the point. (If you and your partner are of different ability, establish a smaller target area for the better player.)

To Decrease Difficulty

- If necessary, allow the ball to bounce more than once to keep the rally going.

Success Check

- Always keep your eye on the ball.
- Concentrate on accuracy rather than power.
- Circle around your partner.

Score Your Success

Rally for more than 5 minutes on the forehand side= 10 points

Rally for 3 to 5 minutes on the forehand side = 5 points

Rally for less than 3 minutes on the forehand side = 1 point

Rally for more than 5 minutes on the backhand side = 10 points

Rally for 3 to 5 minutes on the backhand side = 5 points

Rally for less than 3 minutes on the backhand side = 1 point

Your score ____

Moving and Hitting in the Backcourt Drill 5.
Backcourt Game

Play a conditioned, or modified, game in which you and your opponent must hit shots that bounce past the back of the service box. Play the game with point-per-rally scoring to 11 points. Play three games.

To Increase Difficulty

- Allow your opponent to hit any shot, but you must hit your shots past the back of the service box.

To Decrease Difficulty

- Allow one shot per player per rally to bounce in front of the short line.

Success Check

- Cut out shots that may die in the back corners.
- Hit high on the front wall when under pressure.
- Hit with good width and depth to stop your opponent from cutting off your shots.

Score Your Success

Win two out of three games against your opponent = 5 points

Win one out of three games against your opponent = 3 points

Your score ___

Moving and Hitting in the Backcourt Drill 6.
Two-Ball Feeds

Have two feeders, each with a ball, stand on the short line. The feeders feed alternate straight drives to your forehand and backhand sides. Stand at the back of the court and move from side to side, hitting straight drives (figure 4.10). Time how long you can hit drives continuously without a miss.

To Increase Difficulty

- Have the feeders feed more quickly so that you must move across the court faster to hit your shots.
- Have one feeder hit a straight drive and the other hit a straight drop (a short shot to the frontcourt). Run diagonally across the court, between the feeders, and hit a straight drive from the back and then a straight drive from the front.

To Decrease Difficulty

- Have the feeders wait until you are set up before feeding you the ball.

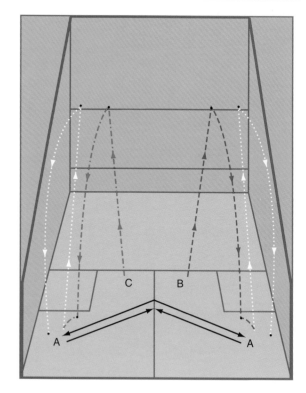

Figure 4.10 Two-ball feeds.

Success Check

- Hit the ball with your body turned slightly toward the back corner.
- Keep your hips still as you swing.
- Move smoothly across the court.

Score Your Success

Hit drives continuously for more than 5 minutes = 10 points

Hit drives continuously for 3 to 5 minutes = 5 points

Hit drives continuously for less than 3 minutes = 1 point

Your score ___

SUCCESS SUMMARY OF MOVING AND HITTING IN THE BACKCOURT

Hitting in the backcourt is without doubt the toughest aspect of the game. To get in good position, either wait for the ball to bounce as far off the back wall as possible or cut off the ball before it hits the back wall. Always use traditional movement on the backhand side and on the forehand side if the ball is bouncing off the back wall or you can step forward into the shot. Use dynamic movement on the forehand side if you are cutting off the ball before it hits the back wall and are stepping back to the ball. By mastering this area of the court, you'll limit your opponent's main means of attack. Ask another player to evaluate your skills in moving and hitting in the backcourt using figures 4.3 through 4.5.

Before moving on to step 5, Volleys, evaluate how you did on the drills in this step. Tally your scores to determine how well you have mastered correct backcourt movement and hitting. If you scored 60 points or more, you are ready to move on to step 5. If you did not score at least 60 points, practice the drills again until you raise your scores before moving on to step 5.

Moving and Hitting in the Backcourt Drills

1. Drives From the Back Corner	___ out of 10
2. Continuous Drives	___ out of 10
3. Backcourt Drives on the Run	___ out of 20
4. Backcourt Rallying	___ out of 20
5. Backcourt Game	___ out of 5
6. Two-Ball Feeds	___ out of 10
Total	___ **out of 75**

Now that you have learned how to put the basic swing together with court movement in the front and the back of the court, it is time to start introducing some other shots. Step 5 covers the volley, in which you hit the ball before it bounces on the floor. Volleying will help you to attack your opponent and also save you from having to try to retrieve some difficult shots that, if you let them bounce, would end up in the back corners.

Volleys

Volleying is one of the most important elements of squash. When players step up to take the ball on the volley, they speed up the game and stretch their opponents to the limit. A good volleyer dominates the T, punishing any shot that the opponent doesn't hit tight to the side walls.

The volley is a shot that is hit before the ball bounces. Players often use the volley around the middle of the court to cut off an opponent's shot before it reaches the back. It can also be hit from the back of the court off an opponent's lob or to return a serve.

At first, you should work on hitting volleys deep into the back of the court because this is a higher-percentage shot than a volley to the front of the court. As your volleying becomes more consistent, vary your volleys more and hit some volley drops and kills. Steps 8 and 9 cover these shots.

Whenever possible, hit an attacking volley with plenty of pace and good width and depth.

This will pressure your opponent and keep the advantage you've gained by taking the ball early. It will sometimes be necessary, however, to hit a soft, high defensive volley with the sole aim of maneuvering your opponent into one of the back corners.

Volleying is important for several reasons. First, taking the ball on the volley often helps you avoid playing more difficult shots from the back of the court. It also saves energy, cutting down on the running you have to do to retrieve the ball from the back of the court. Moreover, it helps reduce the time your opponent has to recover after hitting a shot. This last reason is probably the most important, especially as you become better at handling shots from the back corners. In tight matches, the player who steps up and takes the initiative by volleying often comes out on top. To be a good volleyer, you need to have the confidence to step across quickly and take the ball early.

FOREHAND VOLLEY

You should be ready to use either traditional or dynamic movement when hitting the forehand volley. If the ball is coming slowly, use traditional movement as you step into the shot with your front foot to generate power. If the ball is coming at you quickly, use dynamic movement. Take a quick step across with your back foot, and punch your volley with a short swing.

Preparation is important with the volley. You need time to concentrate on the way you strike the ball. While waiting for your opponent's shot, keep your racket face up rather than down by your feet. Then, when your opponent strikes the ball and you see the direction it's going, bring your racket back to be ready for your shot (figures 5.1*a* and 5.2*a*). Keep your wrist cocked and your elbow slightly bent. Use a slightly shorter backswing than you use for the forehand drive so you can hit the ball with more control. If the ball is coming at you slowly, step across with your front foot and turn your front shoulder so that your shoulders are facing the back corner. If the ball is coming at you fast, step across with your back foot. Still try to turn your front shoulder, but this time your shoulders will face the side wall.

Strike the ball level with your front shoulder when hitting a straight volley and slightly farther forward for a crosscourt volley. Keep your wrist firm, and punch or push through the ball (figures 5.1*b* and 5.2*b*). As with the drive, you should hit with an open racket face to help you hit high enough on the front wall to get the ball to the back of the court. Swing through faster if you are using traditional movement to generate power. If you are using dynamic movement, swing slower and punch the ball higher on the front wall.

Follow through in the intended direction of your shot (figures 5.1*c* and 5.2*c*). Use a more compact follow-through than the one you use for the forehand drive. Also, make sure that you keep your hips and feet still until you've finished the shot.

Figure 5.1   Forehand Volley With Traditional Movement

a

b

PREPARATION

1. Bring racket back early
2. Turn shoulders
3. Use short backswing
4. Keep wrist cocked
5. Keep elbow bent
6. Step across on front foot

EXECUTION

1. Keep wrist firm and cocked
2. Strike ball level with front shoulder
3. Punch through ball

FOLLOW-THROUGH

1. Keep feet still
2. Keep hips still
3. Follow through in intended direction of shot

c

 Misstep
Your volley lacks power.

Correction
Grip the racket a bit more firmly, and keep your wrist firm as you push through the shot.

Figure 5.2   Forehand Volley With Dynamic Movement

PREPARATION

1. Bring racket back early
2. Use short backswing
3. Turn shoulder so body faces side wall
4. Keep wrist cocked
5. Keep elbow bent
6. Step across on back foot

a

(continued)

Figure 5.2   *(continued)*

b

c

EXECUTION

1. Keep wrist firm and cocked
2. Strike ball level with front shoulder
3. Punch through ball

FOLLOW-THROUGH

1. Keep feet still
2. Keep hips still
3. Follow through in intended direction of shot

Misstep
You have no time to hit a volley.

Correction
Watch carefully as your opponent hits the ball, and prepare your racket early. Use dynamic movement if the ball is coming at you quickly on the forehand side.

BACKHAND VOLLEY

It is always best to use traditional movement on the backhand side unless the ball is coming at you so fast that you have no choice but to take a quick step with your back foot and hit a reaction shot.

Early preparation is just as important for the backhand volley as it is for the forehand volley. Bring your wrist up so that your racket face goes behind the back of your head (figure 5.3*a*). Keep your wrist cocked and your knuckles facing up. Step across on your front foot, and turn your front shoulder toward the side wall.

Strike the ball slightly farther forward of your front shoulder with your racket face open (figure 5.3*b*). Your wrist should stay firm throughout the shot, and you should punch through the ball. As with the forehand, when hitting crosscourt, take the ball early, striking it even farther forward than your front shoulder.

Keep the follow-through more compact than you do when hitting the backhand drive, but bring the racket face up in a similar manner (figure 5.3*c*). Your hips and feet should stay still until you've finished the shot.

Figure 5.3 | Backhand Volley

a

b

PREPARATION

1. Keep racket face behind head
2. Cock wrist
3. Keep knuckles facing up
4. Turn front shoulder toward side wall
5. Step across on front foot

EXECUTION

1. Keep wrist firm
2. Hold racket face open
3. Make contact slightly farther forward than your front shoulder
4. Punch through ball

c

FOLLOW-THROUGH

1. Keep feet still
2. Keep hips still
3. Follow through in intended direction of shot

Misstep
Your volley lacks depth.

Correction
Open the racket face more so that you can hit higher on the front wall. Also, keep your wrist firm.

FOREHAND VOLLEY FROM DEEP IN THE COURT

Often you will have to hit a volley from near the back wall, usually following an opponent's serve or lob shot. If you don't volley in this situation, the ball will die in the back corner, giving you no chance to return it. Generally, the deeper you are in the court, the more defensive your volley should be. On the forehand side, use traditional movement if the ball is coming at you slowly and dynamic movement if it is coming at you fast. Typically, you should use dynamic movement on volleys at the back if you are returning a serve that was hit hard.

When using traditional movement, concentrate on turning sideways (figure 5.4a) and punching through the ball. Keep your racket face up, your wrist cocked, and your elbow slightly bent. Make sure you bend your knees slightly for balance. As you swing, watch the ball carefully onto the racket face (figure 5.4b). Remember that the power comes from the backswing, not from throwing your body into the shot. Strike the ball level with your front shoulder if you are hitting a straight shot or slightly forward from your front shoulder if you are hitting a crosscourt shot. Keep your body and feet still and control your follow-through as well as you can (figure 5.4c). Finally, give yourself plenty of room to swing, particularly if you're volleying the ball after it hits the side wall.

Misstep
You mis-hit the volley.

Correction
Make sure that you watch the ball carefully onto the racket face.

Misstep
You hit a straight volley that goes down the middle of the court.

Correction
This is probably caused by hitting too soon. Wait for the ball to come to the side of your body.

Figure 5.4 **Forehand Volley From Deep in the Court, Traditional Movement**

PREPARATION

1. Keep racket face up
2. Cock wrist
3. Keep elbow bent
4. Give yourself plenty of room
5. Turn shoulders toward back corner
6. Step across on front foot

a

b

c

EXECUTION

1. Bend knees
2. Punch through ball

FOLLOW-THROUGH

1. Keep body still
2. Follow through in intended direction of shot
3. Bring racket face up to front shoulder

If the ball is coming at you quickly, use dynamic movement. Step back with your back foot. Turn your shoulders so that your body is facing the side wall (figure 5.5a). Keep your knees bent and punch through the ball (figure 5.5b). Your body should be still as you strike the ball and follow through. Follow through in the intended direction of the shot (figure 5.5c).

Figure 5.5   Forehand Volley From Deep in the Court, Dynamic Movement

a   b   c

PREPARATION

1. Give yourself plenty of room
2. Step across on back foot
3. Turn shoulders toward side wall

EXECUTION

1. Bend knees
2. Punch through ball

FOLLOW-THROUGH

1. Keep body still
2. Follow through in intended direction of shot

BACKHAND VOLLEY FROM DEEP IN THE COURT

On the backhand side, it is always best to step across with your front foot when hitting a volley from deep in the court. Make sure you give yourself plenty of room, especially if the ball is coming off the side wall. Prepare your racket early. Your wrist should be cocked, and your racket face should be around the back of your neck (figure 5.6a). Bring your elbow back as you turn your front shoulder toward the back wall. Step across with your front foot just before you begin to swing. Make sure you keep your knees slightly bent as you swing through (figure 5.6b). Keep your wrist firm throughout the shot and your racket face open. Strike the ball level with your front shoulder if you are hitting the ball straight and slightly forward from your front shoulder if you are hitting crosscourt. Your body should be still as you follow through (figure 5.6c). Follow through in the direction of your shot. Bend your elbow, and then bring your racket face up.

| Figure 5.6 | Backhand Volley From Deep in the Court |

a

b

c

PREPARATION

1. Give yourself plenty of room
2. Turn shoulders toward back corner
3. Hold racket face by back of neck
4. Step across on front foot

EXECUTION

1. Bend knees
2. Punch through ball

FOLLOW-THROUGH

1. Keep body still
2. Follow through in intended direction of shot

Misstep
Your volley lacks control.

Correction
Keep your body still as you strike the ball, and try using a shorter swing.

Volley Drill 1. *Target Volleys*

Set a target against the side wall about 2 feet (0.6 m) behind the back of the service box. Stand on the short line about 6 feet (1.8 m) from the side wall. Hit a soft feed about halfway up the front wall. Volley the ball straight into the back corner. Try to make your volley bounce on the target. Hit 10 forehand volleys and 10 backhand volleys.

To Increase Difficulty

- Move farther back in the court.
- Hit crosscourt volleys to a target in the opposite back corner.

To Decrease Difficulty

- Move forward in the court.

Success Check

- Prepare your racket early.
- Keep your wrist firm.
- Punch through the ball.

Score Your Success

5 to 10 forehand volleys hit the target = 10 points

3 or 4 forehand volleys hit the target = 5 points

1 or 2 forehand volleys hit the target = 1 point

5 to 10 backhand volleys hit the target = 10 points

3 or 4 backhand volleys hit the target = 5 points

1 or 2 backhand volleys hit the target = 1 point

Your score ___

Volley Drill 2. *Continuous Volleys*

Stand on the short line, and continually volley the ball back to yourself. Keep on the balls of your feet, and adjust your feet constantly to position yourself correctly for each volley. See how many consecutive forehand volleys you can hit. Then see how many consecutive backhand volleys you can hit.

To Increase Difficulty

- Move farther back in the court.
- Alternate forehand and backhand volleys.

To Decrease Difficulty

- Move forward in the court.

Success Check

- Prepare your racket quickly.
- Keep your body still as you swing.
- Use a short swing.

Score Your Success

20 or more consecutive forehand volleys = 5 points

15 to 19 consecutive forehand volleys = 3 points

10 to 14 consecutive forehand volleys = 1 point

20 or more consecutive backhand volleys = 5 points

15 to 19 consecutive backhand volleys = 3 points

10 to 14 consecutive backhand volleys = 1 point

Your score ___

Volley Drill 3. *Front Corner Crisscross Volleys*

Stand on the T. Hit a forehand across your body so that it hits the front wall close to the side wall. The ball should rebound off the side wall back to the middle of the court (figure 5.7). Then hit a backhand volley to the opposite front corner so that it hits the front wall, then the side wall, and then returns to the middle. Keep this going as long as you can without the ball hitting the floor. See how many consecutive volleys you can hit.

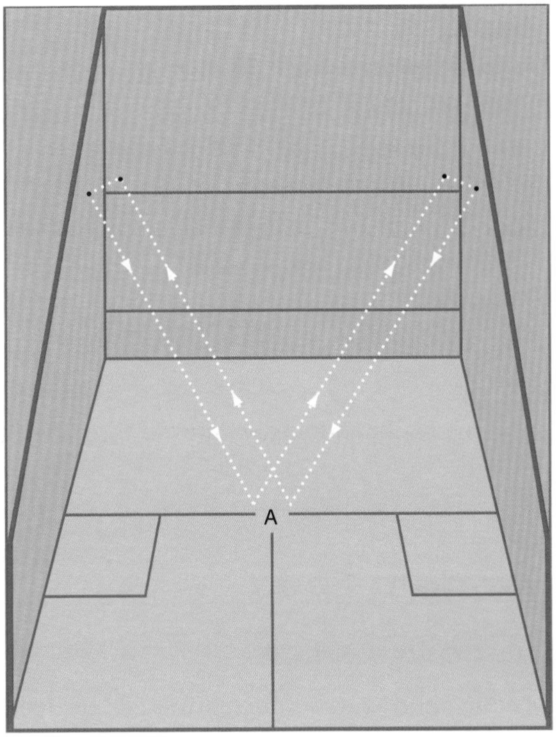

To Increase Difficulty

- Move farther forward in the court.

To Decrease Difficulty

- Let the ball hit the floor to get into a rhythm.

Success Check

- Turn your shoulder as you prepare your racket.
- Hit the shot on the front wall close to the side wall.
- Shuffle your feet to get into the correct position to hit.

Score Your Success

20 or more consecutive volleys = 10 points

15 to 19 consecutive volleys = 5 points

10 to 14 consecutive volleys = 1 point

Your score ___

Figure 5.7 Front corner crisscross volleys.

Volley Drill 4. *Volleys From a Partner's Feed*

Have a partner stand in the back corner and feed you soft, high shots. Step across from the T and hit straight volleys (figure 5.8). If possible, your partner should keep the exercise going without stopping between shots. Try to make the volleys bounce behind the back of the service box and no farther from the side wall than the width of the service box. Hit 10 forehand volleys and 10 backhand volleys.

To Increase Difficulty

- Set a target in the back corner and aim at it.
- Have your partner stand farther forward and hit volleys off your shots.
- On the forehand side, alternate between traditional and dynamic movements.

To Decrease Difficulty

- Have your partner stop after each shot so that you have time to prepare for the next one.

Success Check

- Step across with your front foot.
- Transfer your weight to the front foot as you hit.
- Hit the ball between your body and the side wall.

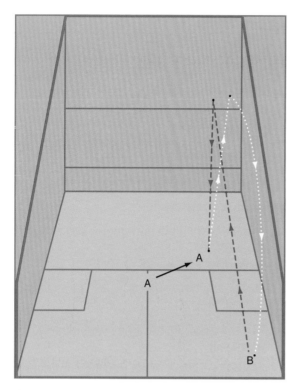

Figure 5.8 Volleys from a partner's feed.

Score Your Success

8 to 10 forehand volleys that bounce behind back of service box = 5 points

6 or 7 forehand volleys that bounce behind back of service box = 3 points

4 or 5 forehand volleys that bounce behind back of service box = 1 point

Your score ____

8 to 10 backhand volleys that bounce behind back of service box = 5 points

6 or 7 backhand volleys that bounce behind back of service box = 3 points

4 or 5 backhand volleys that bounce behind back of service box = 1 point

Your score ____

Volley Drill 5. *Volleys From a Random Feed*

This drill is similar to drill 4, except this time your partner can feed either straight or crosscourt. Again, step across and hit straight volleys. Your partner should keep the exercise going without stopping between shots. Time yourself to see how long you can keep the drill going.

To Increase Difficulty

- Have your partner try to hit volleys off your shots.

To Decrease Difficulty

- Have your partner alternate between straight and crosscourt feeds instead of randomly feeding straight or crosscourt.

Success Check

- Turn and watch your partner as he feeds the ball.
- Prepare your racket early.
- Punch through the ball.

Score Your Success

Keep the drill going for more than 2 minutes = 10 points

Keep the drill going for 1 to 2 minutes = 5 points

Keep the drill going for less than 1 minute = 1 point

Your score ____

Volley Drill 6. *Volleys on the Run*

From a partner's soft, high feed, hit a volley. The volley should bounce behind the back of the service box and no farther from the side wall than the width of the service box. After hitting the volley, turn and run across to touch the opposite side wall before returning to the T for the next volley. Hit 10 forehand volleys and 10 backhand volleys.

To Increase Difficulty

- Have your partner feed faster and lower to make you stretch more and move more quickly.
- Instead of touching the side wall, play an imaginary shot close to the back of the opposite service box.
- Instead of touching the side wall, run backward and touch the back wall between shots.

To Decrease Difficulty

- Have your partner wait for you to return to the T before feeding the ball.

Success Check

- Watch your partner strike the ball.
- Time your movement so that your last step is just before you swing.
- Keep your body still as you punch through.

Score Your Success

8 to 10 forehand volleys that bounce behind the back of the service box = 10 points

6 or 7 forehand volleys that bounce behind the back of the service box = 5 points

4 or 5 forehand volleys that bounce behind the back of the service box = 1 point

8 to 10 backhand volleys that bounce behind the back of the service box = 10 points

6 or 7 backhand volleys that bounce behind the back of the service box = 5 points

4 or 5 backhand volleys that bounce behind the back of the service box = 1 point

Your score ___

Volley Drill 7. *Two-Ball Feeds for Volleys*

Have two feeders, each with a ball, alternate feeding shots for you to volley, one on the forehand side and one on the backhand side. Move from side to side, hitting straight volleys back to the feeders. The feeder should strike the ball just after you have turned from hitting the last volley. As with all volley drills, try to make the ball bounce behind the back of the service box and no farther from the side wall than the width of the service box. See how long you can hit continuous volleys.

To Increase Difficulty

- Have the feeders feed lower and faster.
- On the forehand side, alternate between traditional and dynamic movements.

To Decrease Difficulty

- Have the feeders wait longer before feeding the ball.

Success Check

- Turn toward the front wall after each volley.
- Prepare your racket early.
- Wait on the T for the feeder to feed the ball.

Score Your Success

Volley continuously for more than 5 minutes = 10 points

Volley continuously for 3 to 5 minutes = 5 points

Volley continuously for less than 3 minutes = 1 point

Your score __

Volley Drill 8. *Crosscourt Cutoffs*

Player A stands in a back corner and hits the ball off the side wall to the opposite frontcourt. Player B stands in the opposite front corner and hits a crosscourt drive. You (player C) stand on the T and cut off the crosscourt with a straight volley back to player A (figure 5.9). See how long you can keep the drill going.

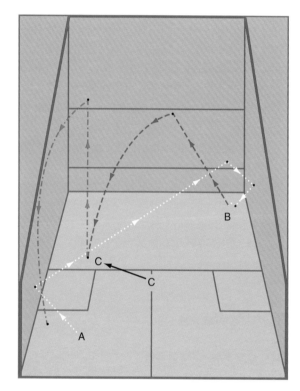

Figure 5.9 Crosscourt cutoffs.

To Increase Difficulty

- Have player B vary the pace, width, and height of the crosscourt shots.
- On the forehand side, alternate between traditional and dynamic movements.

To Decrease Difficulty

- Have player B hit soft crosscourt shots to make volleying easier.

Success Check

- Step across on your front foot.
- Hit the volley between your body and the side wall.
- Keep your wrist firm.

Score Your Success

Keep the drill going for more than 5 minutes hitting forehand volleys = 5 points

Keep the drill going for 3 to 5 minutes hitting forehand volleys = 3 points

Keep the drill going for less than 3 minutes hitting forehand volleys = 1 point

Keep the drill going for more than 5 minutes hitting backhand volleys = 5 points

Keep the drill going for 3 to 5 minutes hitting backhand volleys = 3 points

Keep the drill going for less than 3 minutes hitting backhand volleys = 1 point

Your score ____

Volley Drill 9. *Random Cutoffs*

This drill is similar to drill 8, except player B, at the front of the court, has the option of hitting either crosscourt shots or straight drives. Watch carefully and be ready to volley on either your forehand or backhand side. See how long you can keep the drill going.

To Increase Difficulty

- Have player B vary the pace and height of the straight and crosscourt drives.

To Decrease Difficulty

- Have player B alternate between hitting straight and crosscourt drives.

Success Check

- Watch the ball carefully.
- Prepare your racket quickly.
- Punch the ball.

Score Your Success

Keep the drill going for more than 3 minutes = 10 points

Keep the drill going for 2 to 3 minutes = 5 points

Keep the drill going for less than 2 minutes = 1 point

Your score ___

Volley Drill 10. *Volley Game*

Play a conditioned, or modified, game in which you and your opponent must hit every shot on the volley to the backcourt. You lose a point if you allow the ball to hit the ground beyond the short line or if your shot bounces in front of the short line. Play three games with point-per-rally scoring to 11 points.

To Increase Difficulty

- Your opponent does not have to hit a volley on every shot.

To Decrease Difficulty

- Your opponent also loses the point if his shot hits the back wall before it hits the floor.

Success Check

- Watch the ball.
- Prepare your racket early.
- Move to the T after your shot.

Score Your Success

Win two out of three games against your opponent = 5 points

Win one out of three games against your opponent = 3 points

Your score ___

SUCCESS SUMMARY OF VOLLEYS

When you use it well, the volley speeds up the pace of the match, stretching your opponent to the limit and giving her little time to recover from the previous shot. In tight matches, good volleying often is the key to victory. In addition, the volley helps you avoid more difficult shots out of the back corners, a huge plus for lower-level players. Have a coach check your volleying technique against figures 5.1 through 5.6.

Before moving on to step 6, Serve and Return of Serve, evaluate how you did on the drills in this step. Tally your scores to determine how well you have mastered volleying. If you scored 80 points or more, you are ready to move on to step 6.If you did not score at least 80 points, practice the drills again until you raise your scores before moving on to step 6.

Volley Drills

1. Target Volleys __ out of 20
2. Continuous Volleys __ out of 10
3. Front Corner Crisscross Volleys __ out of 10
4. Volleys From a Partner's Feed __ out of 10
5. Volleys From a Random Feed __ out of 10
6. Volleys on the Run __ out of 20
7. Two-Ball Feeds for Volleys __ out of 10
8. Crosscourt Cutoffs __ out of 10
9. Random Cutoffs __ out of 10
10. Volley Game __ out of 5

Total __ **out of 115**

Now that you have the volley down, you are ready to work on the serve and return of serve. Step 6 introduces various types of serves. It also highlights key points on the return of serve, which involves many of the volley skills you have worked on in this step.

Serve and Return of Serve

When top players serve, they appear to put almost no thought or effort into the shot. Unlike in tennis, the serve in squash rarely wins the point immediately, and thus its importance seems limited. Actually, the serve is often crucial to success in a match. Top players develop a basic serve that they are confident will pressure their opponent. They add to this by perfecting variations of the serve to keep their opponents on their toes and unsure of what to expect.

It's important to take advantage of the serve because it's the only shot you don't have to move to hit. A good serve puts your opponent on the defensive and allows you to control the T immediately. A weak serve, however, gives your opponent the opportunity to attack and take the initiative from you.

The way you return the serve often sets the tone for the rally. If you attack the serve with a shot to the frontcourt, the server often will counterattack. The ensuing rally usually will be short, with many attempted winners. A defensive shot to the back corner often will lead to a longer, drawn-out rally. Therefore, you can use the return of serve to set a tone for the rally that is right for you.

SERVING FROM THE LEFT BOX

The basic serve from the left box (right box for left-handed players) is similar to the basic forehand drive. Begin by facing the opposite side wall with your back foot completely in the box and your racket up and ready to hit a forehand (figure 6.1a). Step across with your front foot while throwing the ball toward the opposite side wall. Be careful not to throw the ball too high because this will make it difficult to time the swing. Also, be sure to throw the ball about 3 to 4 feet (1 to 1.2 m) away from

your body so that you aren't cramped when swinging. A good way of approaching this is to stretch out your arm fully and just let the ball roll off your fingers.

Remember that when you serve, you must strike the ball before it bounces. As you step across to hit, turn your front shoulder slightly toward the opposite back corner and let the ball drop to between waist and knee height before swinging (figure 6.1b). Swing as you would for a forehand drive, keeping the wrist cocked and pushing through the ball. Control your swing and don't try to hit the ball too hard—you'll only waste energy and hit a less accurate shot.

After striking the ball, move smoothly to the T, keeping your eye on the ball as it travels toward the back corner (figure 6.1c).

Figure 6.1　Basic Serve From the Left Box

a

b

c

PREPARATION

1. Face opposite side wall
2. Keep back foot in box
3. Hold racket up ready for a forehand

EXECUTION

1. Step across with front foot
2. Throw ball out toward T
3. Let ball drop to waist height
4. Keep wrist firm
5. Keep hips still

FOLLOW-THROUGH

1. Step toward T
2. Watch ball

Misstep
Your serve does not reach the short line.

Correction
Step into the serve to get more power. Let the ball drop lower so that you can use a full swing.

Aim your serve slightly to the right of the center on the front wall, about two-thirds of the way up. More important, though, the ball should hit the side wall toward the back of the service box at about the point where your opponent would try to cut it off (figure 6.2). Make sure you hit the ball hard enough and high enough so that it bounces on the floor close to the back wall. Ideally, your serve should be too difficult for your opponent to hit straight and should force a return off the side wall to the frontcourt. Make sure that you keep your wrist firm and your body still as you swing through. Too much movement with your hips will make you hit the ball too high and to the right, causing the ball to go out of court on the side wall.

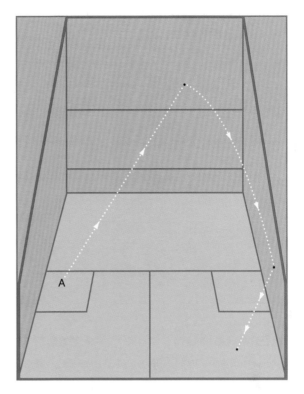

Figure 6.2 Ball path for the serve from the left box.

Misstep
Your serve goes out of court.

Correction
Hit the serve with less power and aim lower on the front wall.

SERVING FROM THE RIGHT BOX

For the right side (the left side for left-handed players), we describe two serves—a basic serve and a more advanced serve, which you should start to work on when you're comfortable with the basic serve. Begin by facing the side wall nearer you with your back foot in the box and your racket prepared for a forehand (figure 6.3a). This time throw the ball out to your side but slightly in front of your body to contact the ball in front of you. As you throw, take a small step forward with your front foot, let the ball drop to between waist and knee height, and then swing through (figure 6.3b). Keep your wrist firm and body still. Think also about hitting underneath the ball to get some height on the shot. Immediately after you've struck the ball, begin to move to the T (figure 6.3c).

| Figure 6.3 | Basic Serve From the Right Box |

a

b

c

PREPARATION

1. Face side wall nearer you
2. Keep back foot in box
3. Hold racket up ready for forehand

EXECUTION

1. Take small step forward with front foot
2. Throw ball slightly in front and to side
3. Hit as if hitting a cross-court forehand

FOLLOW-THROUGH

1. Watch ball
2. Move quickly toward T

The ball should hit the center of the front wall about two-thirds of the way up so that it hits the side wall toward the back of the service box (figure 6.4).

With some practice, you should be able to hit a reasonably consistent tight serve with the basic serve from the right box. The basic serve has some problems, however, the biggest of which is that stepping forward means that your momentum is not going toward the T. You must, therefore, move quickly toward the middle so that you're in position when your opponent returns the serve.

An improvement on the basic serve is to step with your front foot across toward the T and turn your body to an open position instead of stepping forward. Start in the same position as for the basic serve (figure 6.5a), but then throw the ball more to the side of your body. Drag the ball across the court with the momentum of your body as you move toward the T (figure 6.5b).

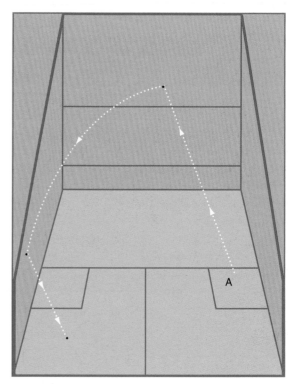

Figure 6.4 Ball path for the serve from the right box.

Figure 6.5	Advanced Serve From the Right Box

a

b

PREPARATION

1. Face side wall nearer you
2. Keep back foot in box
3. Hold racket up ready for a forehand

EXECUTION

1. Throw ball to side of body
2. Step sideways toward T
3. Turn body as you strike the ball
4. Move to T as you follow through

The difficult motion of the advanced serve requires plenty of practice. It's often helpful to work at it in stages. Stand in an open position with your body facing the front wall. Work only on throwing the ball up to your side and hitting it toward the center of the front wall. Transferring the weight from your back foot to your front foot as you do this will help keep your body movement smooth throughout the shot. Once you feel comfortable with this, face the side wall and then step across with your front foot to get to the open position with your body facing forward.

VARYING THE SERVE

The serves described to this point are stock serves that you'll use about 75 percent of the time. Work hard on them to develop consistency. Keep in mind, however, that it may be advantageous to adapt your stock serve according to how your opponent deals with it. If your opponent is stepping forward and volleying your serve before it hits the side wall, aim farther across the front wall to make sure the ball hits the side wall first. This will make attacking your serve much harder. On the other hand, if your opponent makes few attempts to volley your serve and instead lets most of them go to the back, adjust your aim to make the ball hit the side closer to the back corner. This will increase your chances of the ball taking an awkward bounce out of one of the nicks (the cracks between the walls and the floor).

Misstep
Your opponent cuts off your serve with an attacking volley.

Correction
Make sure that your serve hits the side wall. Alternatively, this is the ideal time to use a hard serve down the middle of the court.

Besides your stock serve, you should have some variations to throw in occasionally to keep your opponent guessing. To use the serve as a weapon, you must be able to make constant adjustments.

Lob Serve

Use a motion similar to that of your stock serve, but use less power and hit more underneath the ball to lift it high on the front wall. Use a slightly shorter backswing for more control. Bend your knees a little more (figure 6.6a) than you do on your stock serve. Aim your shot to hit high in the center of the front wall (figure 6.6b). The ball should hit on the side wall a couple of feet below the out-of-court line and near the back of the service box. The object of the lob serve is to force your opponent to hit a difficult high volley. This serve carries a substantial risk of serving out, however, so use it sparingly.

Figure 6.6　**Lob Serve**

a

b

PREPARATION

1. Stand in same position as for stock serve
2. Use short backswing
3. Bend knees

EXECUTION

1. Throw and step in same way as for stock serve
2. Hit underneath ball
3. Hit with less pace
4. Aim high on front wall

Hard-Hit Serve

For the hard-hit serve (figure 6.7), use a motion similar to what you use for your stock serve, but this time swing through faster and hit a little lower on the front wall. It sometimes helps to strike the ball a little higher in the air as well.

This serve is particularly effective when directed down the middle of the court straight at your opponent's body. The object of the hard-hit serve is to surprise your opponent and force a rushed return from an off-balance position. Don't overuse this shot or you'll lose the element of surprise.

Figure 6.7 **Hard–Hit Serve**

a

b

PREPARATION

1. Stand in same position as for stock serve
2. Keep racket high
3. Throw ball slightly higher than stock serve

EXECUTION

1. Step same way as for stock serve
2. Strike ball higher in air
3. Swing through quickly
4. Hit lower on front wall
5. Aim shot down middle of court

Backhand Serve

The backhand serve is useful from the right box (the left box for a left-handed player), but has very few advantages from the left box. From the right box, using the backhand changes the angle of the serve, often making it easier to keep the ball close to the side wall. It also allows you to see where your opponent is standing for the return and enables you to move smoothly and quickly to the T.

Execute the serve similar to the way you perform a forehand serve from the left side. Begin by facing the opposite side wall with your racket prepared for a backhand (figure 6.8a). Throw the ball out to your side, cross your left arm under your right arm, and step across the court with your front foot. Turn your front shoulder toward the back corner so that you can get some power in the shot from the backswing. Hit the ball the same way you hit a backhand drive (figure 6.8b).

Figure 6.8   Backhand Serve From the Right Box

a

b

PREPARATION

1. Face opposite side wall
2. Prepare with racket face behind head
3. Keep elbow close to body
4. Throw ball underneath right elbow

EXECUTION

1. Turn front shoulder toward back corner
2. Step across on front foot
3. Swing through
4. Keep body still

Serve Drill 1. *Throw and Hit*

The purpose of this drill is to practice the motion of throwing and hitting the ball before it bounces without having to worry about where you are standing or aiming the shot.

Stand in the middle of the court. Throw the ball in the air about 3 to 4 feet (1 to 1.2 m) from your body and hit it against the front wall. Let the ball drop to about waist height before making contact, and hit the ball with a forehand swing. Aim to hit your shot high in the center of the front wall.

To Increase Difficulty

- Aim your shots to hit above the service line and bounce past the short line.
- Stand in the service box and hit the ball into the opposite back quarter of the court.

To Decrease Difficulty

- Stand closer to the front wall and use a shorter backswing.

Success Check

- Use a forehand swing.
- Let the ball drop to waist height.
- Watch the ball onto the racket face.

Score Your Success

10 consecutive hits against the front wall = 5 points

Your score ___

Serve Drill 2. *Basic Serve Practice*

On your own, practice hitting basic serves from both the left and right service boxes. Consider a successful serve one that hits the side wall at or behind the back of the service box. Hit 10 serves from the right box and 10 serves from the left box.

Success Check

- Prepare the racket before throwing the ball.
- Take a small step before swinging.
- Strike the ball as you would the forehand.

Score Your Success

8 to 10 successful serves from the right box = 5 points

6 or 7 successful serves from the right box = 3 points

4 or 5 successful serves from the right box = 1 point

8 to 10 successful serves from the left box = 5 points

6 or 7 successful serves from the left box = 3 points

4 or 5 successful serves from the left box = 1 point

Your score ___

Serve Drill 3. *Advanced Serve Practice*

On your own, practice hitting advanced serves from the right service box. Remember to begin by facing the side wall nearer you with your back foot in the box. Work on turning your body to an open position and stepping across with your front foot toward the T as you strike the ball. Consider a successful serve one that hits the front wall and then the side wall at or behind the back of the service box. Hit 10 advanced serves.

To Decrease Difficulty

- Begin with your body facing the front wall instead of the side wall.

Success Check

- Begin by facing the side wall.
- Step across toward the T.
- Turn your body to the front wall when making contact.

Score Your Success

8 to 10 successful serves = 5 points

6 or 7 successful serves = 3 points

4 or 5 successful serves = 1 point

Your score ___

RETURN OF SERVE

A strong return of serve is crucial in gaining the center of the court and taking the initiative from the server. At lower levels, in which rallies tend to be much shorter, the first few shots in a rally often dictate how the rally is going to play out. For example, the first player to hit a tight shot to the back of the court often wins the rally immediately or is set up for a winning shot by the opponent's weak return. As your level of play improves, you'll find that it becomes increasingly difficult to win a rally with one good shot, and that a combination of good shots is necessary. Nevertheless, the return of serve is important because it may be the only shot in the rally for which you have plenty of time to prepare. It's a good opportunity to begin the series of good shots necessary to win the rally.

When returning the serve, you have three basic options: you can go for an attacking shot at the front of the court, hit more defensively into the back corner, or boast the ball to the front of the court (see step 7). The first option is a low-percentage option. You should play it only if the serve is very weak or if you're feeling particularly confident with your attacking shot. The second option usually is preferable, but if this isn't possible because the serve was very good, the last option may be the only way to keep the ball in play.

Most of the time you should look to hit to the back corners. Try to volley the serve straight down the wall, either before or after the ball hits the side wall. The only exception to this is if the serve is overhit and you're confident it will bounce a long way off the back wall. In this case, waiting is often better because it gives you time to set up and thus choose from many options. If the serve is overhit to such a degree that the ball hits the side wall and then the back wall before hitting the floor, give yourself plenty of room to hit your shot. The ball is likely to move a long way out into the middle of the court, so you should back up, forcing your opponent back, which should give you a wide lane to hit a straight drive into the back corner.

Misstep
Your opponent's serve is dying in the back corner.

Correction
Make every effort to volley the serve.

If you're poorly positioned to hit the ball straight, particularly if you step forward to hit a volley but end up hitting the ball in front of you, it's best to hit a deep crosscourt shot. Attempting to hit the volley straight normally leads to a poor return that comes straight back to you. Make sure your crosscourt return is high and wide enough so that your opponent can't volley easily. Aim to hit the opposite side wall near the back of the service box.

When you're waiting to return the serve, it's best to stand slightly behind and to the side of the service box opposite the server. Have your racket up ready for a forehand on the forehand side (figure 6.9a) or a backhand on the backhand side (figure 6.9b). Turn your head and watch the ball as your opponent serves.

As the ball hits the front wall, begin to turn your body to a more sideways position and extend your racket back even farther. Shuffle your feet to

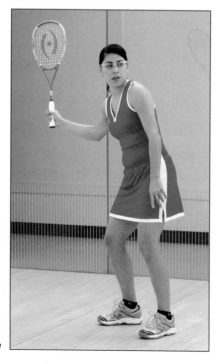

Figure 6.9 Waiting position: *(a)* forehand return of serve; *(b)* backhand return of serve.

get into the best position to strike the ball. Be sure to give yourself enough room to swing through comfortably. Hit the ball to the side of your body, keeping your wrist firm as you swing through.

Follow through in the direction you want the ball to go. Your hips and feet should stay still until you have finished the follow-through. Once you've completed the stroke, move smoothly to the T. Give your opponent room to move in front of you to the back corner if you've hit the ball deep and straight.

Misstep
Your return of serve goes down the middle of the court.

Correction
Make up your mind early whether to hit the return straight or crosscourt. If you're hitting crosscourt, hit with more width. If you're hitting straight, make sure that you hit your shot to the side of your body.

Most problems with the return of serve are caused by either rushing or trying to be too aggressive with the shot. If you're having trouble with this aspect of your game, be patient and think about just making a solid return that will keep you in the rally.

Return of Serve Drill 1. *Straight Volley Returns*

Have a partner hit a high crosscourt from the front corner (figure 6.10a). Hit a straight volley from the back, and then hit a shot off the side wall back to your partner in the front corner (figure 6.10b). Your partner should aim the crosscourt shots to hit high on the side wall close to the back of the service box as a good serve would. Your volleys should bounce behind the back of the service box, no farther from the side wall than the width of the service box. Hit 10 forehand volleys and 10 backhand volleys.

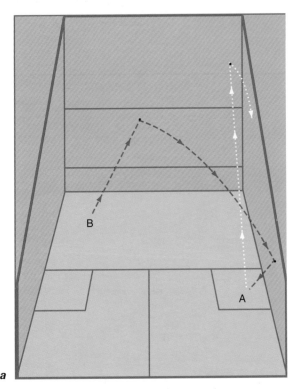

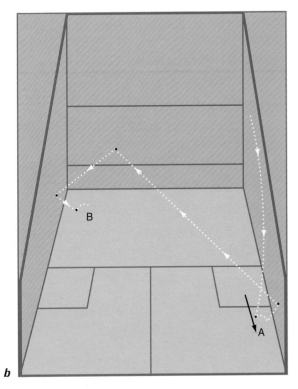

Figure 6.10 Straight volley returns: *(a)* a high crosscourt shot from the front corner followed by a straight volley; *(b)* a shot off the side wall and back to the partner in the front corner.

Success Check

- Stand facing the side wall.
- Hit the ball between your body and the side wall.
- Hit the ball high on the front wall.

Score Your Success

8 to 10 forehand volleys that bounce behind the back of the service box = 10 points

6 or 7 forehand volleys that bounce behind the back of the service box = 5 points

4 or 5 forehand volleys that bounce behind the back of the service box = 1 point

8 to 10 backhand volleys that bounce behind the back of the service box = 10 points

6 or 7 backhand volleys that bounce behind the back of the service box = 5 points

4 or 5 backhand volleys that bounce behind the back of the service box = 1 point

Your score ___

Return of Serve Drill 2.   Crosscourt Volley Returns

With a partner, stand on opposite sides of the court at the back of the service boxes. Hit high crosscourt volleys to each other (figure 6.11). Keep a rally going with your partner without the ball touching the floor.

To Increase Difficulty

- Keep the rally going without stepping in front of the back of the service box.

To Decrease Difficulty

- Let the ball bounce to keep the rally going.

Success Check

- Keep your wrist firm.
- Punch through the ball.
- Hit with plenty of width.

Score Your Success

Rally 30 shots or more = 10 points

Rally 20 to 29 shots = 5 points

Rally 19 shots or fewer = 1 point

Your score ___

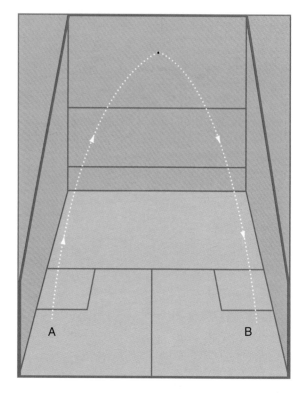

Figure 6.11 Crosscourt volley returns.

Return of Serve Drill 3. *Serve and Rally Game*

Work with a partner. One player serves and the other returns the serve with a straight volley or drive (figure 6.12*a*). After the return of serve, continue playing a rally, hitting only straight drives (figure 6.12*b*). At first, practice with your partner without keeping score. Then play a conditioned, or modified, game in which every shot must bounce past the short line but no farther than service-box width from the side wall. Play three games using point-per-rally scoring to 11 points.

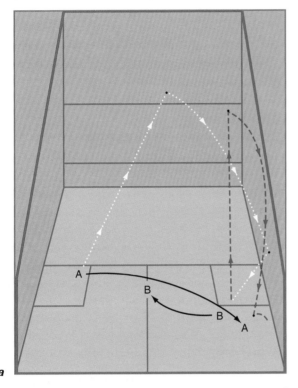
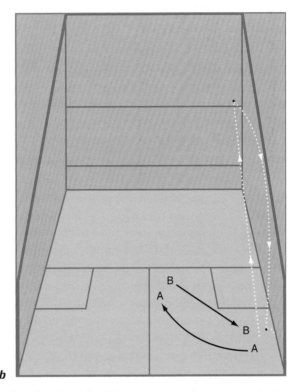

Figure 6.12 Serve and rally game: *(a)* serve and return of serve; *(b)* rally of straight drives.

To Increase Difficulty

- Make the target area smaller; that is, every shot must bounce behind the back of the service box.

Success Check

- Make the serve hit the side wall.
- Volley the return of serve whenever possible.
- Circle around each other when hitting straight drives.

Score Your Success

Win two games against your partner = 5 points

Win one game against your partner = 3 points

Your score ___

Return of Serve Drill 4. *Serve and Crosscourt Rally Game*

Work with a partner. One player serves and the other returns the serve with a crosscourt shot. Rally crosscourt until one of you hits a shot that bounces outside the opposite back quarter of the court. Play three of these conditioned, or modified, games using point-per-rally scoring to 11 points.

To Increase Difficulty

• Play a game in which you and your partner must volley. You lose a point if you allow a shot to bounce into the target area.

Success Check

• Volley whenever possible.
• Prepare your racket early.
• Hit the ball high on the front wall.

Score Your Success

Win two games against your partner = 5 points
Win one game against your partner = 3 points
Your score ___

SUCCESS SUMMARY FOR SERVE AND RETURN OF SERVE

Begin by learning the basic serves from the right and left boxes. Then mix it up a bit with variations to keep your opponent guessing. Keeping in mind the basics of the forehand swing—racket up, wrist firm, and body still—will help on serves from both sides. Have your coach critique your serve using figures 6.1, 6.3, and 6.5 through 6.8.

To return a serve, you may either hit an attacking shot in the frontcourt, a defensive shot into the back corners, or a boast to the front corner. Volleying the serve will limit your opponent's preparation time, but if the serve is overhit, you may want to let the ball bounce off the back wall.

Try to hit the ball straight, and be sure to allow yourself plenty of room to hit the ball, regardless of its position. Always be prepared with your racket up from the time your opponent begins the serve, and always keep your eye on the ball.

Before moving on to step 7, Boasts, evaluate how you did on the drills in this step. Tally your scores to determine how well you have mastered serves and returns of serve. If you scored 50 points or more, you are ready to move on to step 7. If you did not score at least 50 points, practice the drills again until you raise your scores before moving on to step 7.

Serve Drills

1. Throw and Hit	___ out of 5
2. Basic Serve Practice	___ out of 10
3. Advanced Serve Practice	___ out of 5

Return of Serve Drills

1. Straight Volley Returns	___ out of 20
2. Crosscourt Volley Returns	___ out of 10
3. Serve and Rally Game	___ out of 5
4. Serve and Crosscourt Rally Game	___ out of 5
Total	___ *out of 60*

To this point you have worked only on hitting shots directly onto the front wall. One of the interesting aspects of squash is the angles that come into play by hitting the ball off a side wall onto the front wall. This shot is known as a boast. The boast can be used as a defensive shot to retrieve a ball hit deep into the back corners or as an offensive shot to work your opponent to the front of the court. Step 7 introduces the basic boast shot as well as its variations.

Boasts

The walls of the court dramatically increase the variation of shots you can use in a squash match. They create the opportunity to hit angle shots off the side or back walls to the frontcourt, which allows you to escape some tricky situations in the back corners. In addition, you can attack your opponents with these angles, stretching them to the front corners.

A shot hit off one of the side walls or the back wall onto the front wall is called a boast. There are a variety of boasts, including the trickle boast, skid boast, reverse angle, and back-wall boast, to name but a few.

Most top players use the boast sparingly at the beginning of the match, choosing instead to pin their opponent back with drives and volleys, and playing the boast only when necessary to hit the ball out of the back corners. As the game progresses, however, and their opponent becomes more tired, they begin to work their opponent to the front of the court. The boast, at this stage, becomes a potent offensive weapon.

The boast is a versatile shot. You can hit it from anywhere in the court, and you can use it to attack, to defend, to deceive an unsuspecting opponent, or, as a last-resort shot, to keep you in the rally. For the novice player the boast is the easiest way to hit the ball to the front of the court. The drop shot requires developing good touch, which takes practice to master. The boast, on the other hand, is like hitting a drive into the side wall, and is therefore relatively easy once you can consistently hit a good drive.

As you start playing better players, you'll find that they'll begin to read your boasts more easily and will look to counterattack off them. This doesn't mean you should rule out the boast as an attacking shot, but it will require more disguise. You should play it only if you think your opponent is not watching carefully enough or is out of position and will struggle to retrieve it. Boasting the ball involves a fair amount of risk. A poorly hit boast will often end up in the tin or in a good position for your opponent.

The boast is most useful, however, as an easier way of hitting shots out of the back corners. When your opponent hits a drive to a good length, the ball sometimes is not going to bounce far enough away from the back wall for you to hit a drive. In these situations all you can do is hit the ball off the side wall (in extreme situations, the back wall) and onto the front wall.

BOASTS OUT OF BACK CORNERS

When hitting the boast out of the back corners, use a midstance in the same way as you would for the drive. Your feet should be about shoulder-width apart, with your body turned farther toward the back wall than it would be for the drive (figures 7.1*a* and 7.2*a*). Prepare your racket early and bend your knees because you'll be hitting the ball quite close to the floor.

Make sure that you don't set up too close to the back corner. Give yourself enough room so that you don't hamper your swing. Make contact with the ball out by your front foot, and hit the shot just as you would a drive into the side wall (figures 7.1*b* and 7.2*b*).

As you follow through, make sure that you keep your wrist firm and your racket face open. Abbreviate your follow-through slightly from your drive follow-through so that you get more of a punch at the end of the shot (figures 7.1*c* and 7.2*c*).

Figure 7.1   Forehand Boast Out of the Back Corner

PREPARATION

1. Prepare racket early
2. Cock wrist
3. Keep elbow slightly bent
4. Turn toward back corner
5. Use midstance
6. Bend knees

a

b

c

EXECUTION

1. Hit out by front foot
2. Keep racket face open
3. Keep wrist firm

FOLLOW-THROUGH

1. Push through ball
2. Keep racket face open
3. Bring racket face up
4. Abbreviate follow-through slightly

Misstep
The ball doesn't reach the front wall.

Correction
Don't hit the ball from quite as far behind you, and aim your shot farther along the side wall and closer to the front wall.

Figure 7.2   Backhand Boast Out of the Back Corner

PREPARATION

1. Prepare racket early
2. Hold racket face by back of neck
3. Keep elbow close to body
4. Point elbow down
5. Turn toward back corner
6. Use midstance
7. Bend knees

a

EXECUTION

1. Hit out by front foot
2. Keep knuckles facing up
3. Keep wrist firm

b

FOLLOW-THROUGH

1. Push through ball
2. Keep racket face open
3. Bring racket face up
4. Soften elbow slightly
5. Abbreviate follow-through slightly

c

Imagine another court next to yours, and aim the ball toward the opposite front corner of that court. This will give you the correct angle to make the ball rebound off the side wall onto the front wall within a couple of feet of the opposite side wall. Ideally, after hitting the front wall, the ball should bounce close to the side-wall nick.

The primary purpose of this shot is to take your opponent away from the T and up to the front corner. Don't worry about whether the ball hits the floor first or the side wall first after it hits the front wall. Keep the ball as low as you can without risking hitting the tin; remember that the boast is a defensive shot intended to keep you in the rally, so don't be too ambitious!

It isn't advisable to hit the shot too hard either, because this will result in a less accurate shot that bounces out into the middle of the court. Often, a softer shot will float nicely up into the front corner, giving you time to position yourself on the T for your opponent's return.

If the ball is close not only to the back wall but also to the side wall, use a short backswing and just try to jam the ball out off the side wall. Avoid using any follow-through because you might double-hit the ball (hit the ball a second time as it rebounds off the side wall). Keep the racket face open to make sure the ball goes upward to increase its chances of reaching the front wall.

BOAST FROM THE MIDDLE OF THE COURT

The boast from the middle of the court often is a reflex shot played when cutting off a drive and usually is played on the volley. On the backhand side you should try to get your front foot across; however, as with other reflex shots on the forehand side, it is normally more efficient to use dynamic movement and hit off the back foot. You should aim this shot to come off the side wall and hit low in the middle of the front wall so that its second bounce on the floor is close to the side wall.

Early preparation is key to this shot (figure 7.3a). You should also keep your wrist firm and punch through the ball (figure 7.3b). The shot often requires only a short swing and not much pace on the ball. This is particularly true if your opponent hits a hard shot; in that case your boast is almost a block. If your opponent's shot is softer, punch through a little more quickly to reduce the time your opponent has to get to the front of the court to retrieve the shot. Always concentrate on keeping your swing controlled; in particular, avoid rolling over your wrist as you strike the ball, which may cause it to go into the tin.

Misstep
The ball hits the tin.

Correction
Keep your racket face open so that you strike under the ball. Aim higher on the side wall, particularly from defensive positions.

| Figure 7.3 | **Boast From the Middle of the Court** |

PREPARATION

1. Prepare racket early
2. Step across on back foot
3. Turn front shoulder toward side wall
4. Keep wrist firm

a

EXECUTION

1. Punch through ball
2. Keep racket face open
3. Keep body still
4. Use a short swing

b

Misstep
The ball bounces into the middle of the court.

Correction
Hit the ball with less power, and don't aim the shot as far along the side wall.

BOAST FROM THE FRONT OF THE COURT

The boast from the front of the court, normally referred to as a trickle boast, is played from one of the front corners of the court. Try to hit this shot with plenty of disguise. Position yourself and shape up with a big backswing as if you were going to hit a hard drive (figure 7.4a). Then, as you bring the racket face down to make contact with the ball, keep your wrist forward instead of pushing your racket face through (figure 7.4b). Leading with your wrist in this manner will keep the racket face facing toward the side wall as you contact the ball.

Figure 7.4   Boast From the Front of the Court

PREPARATION

1. Use big backswing
2. Lead with wrist
3. Hold racket face toward side wall

a

EXECUTION

1. Slice ball
2. Swing through quickly
3. Use short follow-through

b

Misstep
Your opponent hits winners off your boasts.

Correction
Use the shot less frequently so that you increase the element of surprise. When you must boast, hit with less power so that you have more time to recover to the T.

Swing through quite fast but with a shorter follow-through, and slice the ball into the side wall. Keep the ball low to minimize your opponent's chances of retrieving the shot. If the large backswing is believable, your opponent will be on his heels and won't be able to get to the front of the court fast enough to hit the ball before the second bounce. Beware, however, because if your opponent does reach the ball, he will have the whole court to hit into, and you'll be stranded in the front corner. For this reason a drop shot (see step 8) is normally a better attacking shot to play from the front of the court. Only occasionally throw in the trickle boast. Yet, for the lower-level player who hasn't developed good touch with the drop, the trickle boast can be the most effective shot at the front of the court.

BACK-WALL BOAST

The back-wall boast (figure 7.5) is a last-resort shot played when your opponent has hit a shot past you and there is no way you can hit a boast off the side wall. Usually this happens when you are at full stretch and reaching behind you for the ball, or when your opponent's shot comes off the side wall and stays so close to the back wall that you can't hit a boast far enough along the side wall to reach the front wall.

When at full stretch for this shot, just concentrate on getting your racket face underneath the ball. Lift the ball so that, after hitting the back wall, it travels high in the air and then drops onto the front wall. Hit the shot just hard enough to guarantee that the ball reaches the front wall. The less pace you use, the more time you'll give yourself to get positioned on the T to cover your opponent's next shot.

Figure 7.5　Back-Wall Boast

a

b

PREPARATION

1. Face back wall
2. Take large step toward back wall
3. Bend down low

EXECUTION

1. Place racket face underneath ball
2. Use short swing
3. Hit soft, looping shot to front wall

It's best to angle the shot so that, after hitting the back wall, it travels diagonally across the court toward the opposite front corner. This considerably reduces the likelihood that you'll hit the ball out of court on the side wall. It also increases the chances that the ball will hit the front wall and then hug the side wall, making it difficult for your opponent to hit an attacking shot.

If you're hitting a back-wall boast because the ball is tight against the back wall, use a short, punchy backswing with virtually no follow-through. Make sure your racket face is open, and try to jam the ball upward. This difficult shot requires much practice, but it's surprising how often, from a seemingly impossible position, you'll be able to get the ball back into play.

Remember that this shot should be your last option. Don't always rely on it to get the ball back into play. Against a good player you'll be giving your opponent an excellent opportunity to hit a winning shot or to make you work hard to retrieve the next shot.

REVERSE ANGLE

The reverse angle is hit off the side wall farther from you and onto the front wall. This is another shot that, on the forehand side, lends itself well to dynamic rather than traditional footwork. To maintain the element of surprise, attempt the shot only occasionally. If your opponent reads the shot, she may be able to get to the front of the court quickly and gain the initiative. This attacking shot is often most effective when hit from deep in the court with your opponent to your side.

One of the best times to play this shot is when your opponent has overhit a shot and the ball has bounced far from the back wall. Make it look as if you're going to hit a crosscourt shot. Prepare the racket early and wait for the ball to come in front of you before you swing (figure 7.6a). The longer you can wait before hitting the ball, the more likely your opponent will be to be back on her heels, expecting the crosscourt shot. Then whip the ball across the court in front of your opponent (figure 7.6b). The ball should hit the side wall so that it comes back across the court to the opposite front corner after hitting the front wall.

Figure 7.6   Reverse Angle

a

b

PREPARATION

1. Prepare racket early
2. Pause before swinging

EXECUTION

1. Hit ball in front of body
2. Swing across body
3. Hit toward side wall farther from you

You can also play the reverse angle when you're in front of your opponent. Be careful when using it from far up the court because if you hit it too high, your opponent will have a good opportunity to get to the ball and drive it past you to the back of the court. Normally, a straight or crosscourt drop is preferable to a reverse angle from the front of the court.

SKID BOAST

The skid boast (figure 7.7) is the only type of boast that doesn't end up in the frontcourt. Instead, this shot sends the ball to the opposite back corner via the side wall nearer you. To do this, you must aim the ball higher on the side wall and closer to the front wall. The ball should hit high in the center of the front wall and then float to the opposite back corner (figure 7.8). Use a more open racket face to get the necessary height on the shot.

| Figure 7.7 | **Skid Boast** |

PREPARATION

1. Keep racket face open
2. Bend knees
3. Hit underneath ball

a

EXECUTION

1. Aim high on side wall
2. Hit with plenty of pace

b

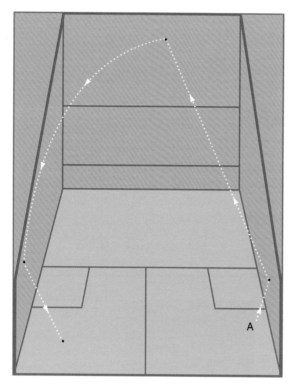

Figure 7.8 Ball path for skid boast.

Use the skid boast sparingly because it is most effective if you can make your opponent move forward, expecting a regular boast. This is a difficult shot to play; you risk giving your opponent an easy opportunity to hit a winner if you don't get the necessary height on the shot. So attempt this shot only when you are well balanced and not under pressure.

Boast Drill 1. *Boasts From a Hand Feed*

Stand near the service box, about 6 feet (1.8 m) from the side wall (figure 7.9*a*). Throw the ball against the side wall. After it bounces, hit a boast toward the opposite front corner (figure 7.9*b*). Try to hit your boast onto the front wall between the service line and the tin. Hit 10 forehand boasts and 10 backhand boasts.

a

b

Figure 7.9 Boasts from a hand feed: *(a)* throw the ball against the side wall; *(b)* hit the boast toward the opposite front corner.

To Increase Difficulty

- Throw the ball against the back wall instead of the side wall.
- Aim at a target on the floor, close to the side wall and about 3 feet (1 m) from the front wall.

To Decrease Difficulty

- Move farther forward in the court.
- Concentrate only on hitting the ball above the tin.

Success Check

- Turn slightly toward the back corner.
- Use a midstance.
- Bend your knees.

Score Your Success

8 to 10 forehand boasts that hit the front wall = 5 points

6 or 7 forehand boasts that hit the front wall = 3 points

4 or 5 forehand boasts that hit the front wall = 1 point

8 to 10 backhand boasts that hit the front wall = 5 points

6 or 7 backhand boasts that hit the front wall = 3 points

4 or 5 backhand boasts that hit the front wall = 1 point

Your score ___

Boast Drill 2. Boasts From a Racket Feed

Stand in the back corner. Hit a straight drive back to yourself, and then hit a boast off your drive (figure 7.10). If possible, hit the drive deep enough so it rebounds off the back wall after hitting the floor. Aim to make the boast bounce on a target about 3 feet (1 m) from the front wall against the side wall. Hit 10 forehand boasts and 10 backhand boasts.

To Increase Difficulty

- Hit a crosscourt drive, and then turn and move to the other back corner and hit a boast.

To Decrease Difficulty

- Hit a soft drive, away from the side and back walls.
- Concentrate only on hitting the boast above the tin.

Success Check

- Hit the drive high on the front wall.
- Prepare your racket quickly.
- Keep your body still as you swing.

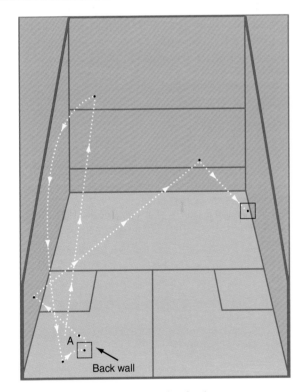

Figure 7.10 Boasts from a racket feed.

Score Your Success

8 to 10 forehand boasts that hit the target =
5 points

6 or 7 forehand boasts that hit the target = 3
points

4 or 5 forehand boasts that hit the target = 1
point

8 to 10 backhand boasts that hit the target =
5 points

6 or 7 backhand boasts that hit the target =
3 points

4 or 5 backhand boasts that hit the target =
1 point

Your score ___

Boast Drill 3. *Crosscourt Drive-Boast Routine*

Have a partner stand in the front corner and hit
crosscourt drives to you in the opposite back
corner (figure 7.11). The crosscourt drives should
hit the side wall, then the floor, and then the back
wall. From a position about 2 feet (0.6 m) behind
the T, move back, turn your body toward the back
corner, and hit a boast back to your partner. Aim
to hit the front wall between the service line and
the tin. After your shot, return to the position just
behind the T for the next crosscourt drive. See
how many consecutive forehand boasts you can
hit above the tin and then how many consecutive
backhand boasts you can hit above the tin.

To Decrease Difficulty

* Have your partner hit soft, high crosscourt
drives that bounce into the middle of the
court.
* Concentrate only on hitting above the tin.

Success Check

* Give yourself plenty of room.
* Turn your body toward the back corner.
* Keep your wrist firm.

Score Your Success

20 or more consecutive forehand boasts above
the tin = 5 points

15 to 19 consecutive forehand boasts above
the tin = 3 points

14 or fewer consecutive forehand boasts above
the tin = 1 point

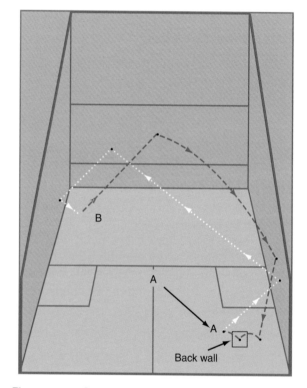

Figure 7.11 Crosscourt drive-boast routine.

20 or more consecutive backhand boasts above
the tin = 5 points

15 to 19 consecutive backhand boasts above
the tin = 3 points

14 or fewer consecutive backhand boasts
above the tin = 1 point

Your score ___

Boast Drill 4. *Drive and Boast*

Put an object on the half-court line about 5 feet (1.5 m) behind the T. Have a partner stand in the frontcourt and hit alternate forehand and backhand straight drives. Stand in the backcourt and hit alternate forehand and backhand boasts (figure 7.12). After each boast, move forward, go around the object, and then return to the corner for the next boast. See how long you can keep the drill going.

To Increase Difficulty

- Move the object closer to the T.

To Decrease Difficulty

- Move the object farther away from the T, or remove the object and just move from side to side.

Success Check

- Sidestep as much as possible.
- Prepare your racket early.
- Keep your feet still as you swing.

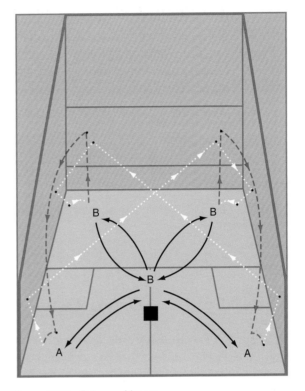

Figure 7.12 Drive and boast.

Score Your Success

Keep the drill going continuously for more than 5 minutes = 10 points

Keep the drill going continuously for 3 to 5 minutes = 5 points

Keep the drill going continuously for less than 3 minutes = 1 point

Your score ___

Boast Drill 5. *Drive and Volley Boast*

This drill is similar to drill 4, except you remove the object from the floor, stand farther forward in the court (about 2 feet [0.6 m] behind the short line), and volley boast your partner's straight drives. See how long you can keep the drill going.

To Increase Difficulty

- Have your partner hit hard, low drives.

Success Check

- Keep your wrist firm.
- Use a short, punchy swing.
- Sidestep across the court.

Score Your Success

Keep the drill going continuously for more than 3 minutes = 10 points

Keep the drill going continuously for 2 to 3 minutes = 5 points

Keep the drill going continuously for less than 2 minutes = 1 point

Your score ___

Boast Drill 6. *Random Boasts*

Have a partner stand in the front corner and hit either straight or crosscourt drives to the back corners. Stand in the backcourt, move into position, and hit boasts from out of the back corners. See how long you can keep the drill going.

To Increase Difficulty

- Allow your partner to hit to any area of the court, while you must hit a boast.

To Decrease Difficulty

- Have your partner alternately hit straight and crosscourt drives.

Success Check

- Don't rush at the ball.
- Carefully watch your opponent strike the ball.

Score Your Success

Keep the drill going for more than 5 minutes = 10 points

Keep the drill going for 3 to 5 minutes = 5 points

Keep the drill going for less than 3 minutes = 1 point

Your score ___

Boast Drill 7. *Drive-Drive-Boast*

Stand on the T with a partner standing in the back corner. Hit a straight drive to your partner, who also hits a straight drive. Move into the back corner and hit a boast. Your partner moves up to the opposite front corner to hit a straight drive. Hit another straight drive. Your partner moves to the back corner to boast. Keep your movement smooth, and try to move through the T. Particularly when moving from the back corner to the opposite front corner, avoid moving across to the side wall too much because this will lead you to approach the ball from behind rather from the side. See how long you can keep the drill going.

Success Check

- Move through the T.
- Volley whenever possible.
- Keep your movement smooth.

Score Your Success

Keep the drill going for more than 5 minutes = 10 points

Keep the drill going for 3 to 5 minutes = 5 points

Keep the drill going for less than 3 minutes = 1 point

Your score ___

Boast Drill 8. *Back Boast, Front Boast*

Have a partner stand in the front corner and hit a straight drive. Hit a boast from the back corner. Your partner then hits a straight drop. Run diagonally across the court to hit a trickle boast from the front. Your partner then drives to the back corner again. Run diagonally to the back corner and boast. When moving back from the front corner, run backward to the T; then turn and move into position for the ball in the backcourt. Hit 20 boasts from the back and 20 boasts from the front of the court on each side.

To Increase Difficulty

- Have your partner hit lower drops and hard, low drives.

To Decrease Difficulty

- Have your partner hit high drop shots to give you plenty of time to move to the front.

Success Check

- Move quickly and smoothly.
- Prepare your racket early.
- Run backward from the front.

20 forehand boasts from the back and 20 backhand boasts from the front = 10 points

10 forehand boasts from the back and 10 backhand boasts from the front = 5 points

20 backhand boasts from the back and 20 forehand boasts from the front = 10 points

10 backhand boasts from the back and 10 forehand boasts from the front = 5 points

Your score ___

Boast Drill 9. *Crosscourt-Boast Rally*

Have one partner (player A) stand in the front corner and another partner (player B) stand on the T while you (player C) stand in the opposite back corner. Player A hits a crosscourt drive and then turns and circles back toward the back corner, staying away from the middle of the court (figure 7.13). Player C, in the back corner, hits a boast and then moves forward to the T. Player B moves forward to the front corner to hit a crosscourt drive off the boast. Once you get into the rhythm of this routine, you'll have no problem remembering which way to move and when it's your turn to hit. To begin with, however, it's easy to be confused and end up in the wrong position. Stay aware of where the ball and your partners are to avoid potentially hazardous situations. See how long you can keep the drill going hitting forehand boasts, and then try the drill hitting backhand boasts.

To Decrease Difficulty

- Hit shots higher to allow more time to move into the correct positions to hit.

Success Check

- Always watch the ball.
- Don't rush.
- Give yourself room to hit.

Keep the drill going hitting forehand boasts for more than 5 minutes = 10 points

Keep the drill going hitting forehand boasts for 3 to 5 minutes = 5 points

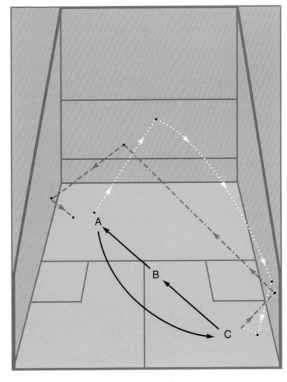

Figure 7.13 Crosscourt-boast rally.

Keep the drill going hitting forehand boasts for less than 3 minutes = 1 point

Keep the drill going hitting backhand boasts for more than 5 minutes = 10 points

Keep the drill going hitting backhand boasts for 3 to 5 minutes = 5 points

Keep the drill going hitting backhand boasts for less than 3 minutes = 1 point

Your score ___

SUCCESS SUMMARY FOR BOASTS

Beginners will find the boast the easiest way to move an opponent to the front of the court. As your game develops and you begin to play better players, you'll find that your opponents look to counterattack off your boast. The boast can still be part of your attacking arsenal, but you'll have to be choosier about when to hit it, and you'll need to hit the boast with more disguise.

For all players, however, the boast will always be an important shot for working the ball out of the back corners. Often it's the only way to return an opponent's shot that is dying close to the back wall. The various types of boasts—the trickle boast, skid boast, back-wall boast, and reverse angle—are hit from different positions on the court. By learning them all, you'll add variety to your game and become a much tougher opponent. Focus at first, however, on the basic boast out of the back corners. Ask someone to critique your boast using figures 7.1 through 7.7.

Before moving on to step 8, Drop and Lob Shots, evaluate how you did on the drills in this step. Tally your scores to determine how well you have mastered boasts. If you scored 85 points or more, you are ready to move on to step 8. If you did not score at least 85 points, practice the drills again until you raise your scores before moving on to step 8.

Boast Drills

1.	Boasts From a Hand Feed	___ out of 10
2.	Boasts From a Racket Feed	___ out of 10
3.	Crosscourt Drive-Boast Routine	___ out of 10
4.	Drive and Boast	___ out of 10
5.	Drive and Volley Boast	___ out of 10
6.	Random Boasts	___ out of 10
7.	Drive-Drive-Boast	___ out of 10
8.	Back Boast, Front Boast	___ out of 20
9.	Crosscourt-Boast Rally	___ out of 20
Total		___ *out of 110*

The boast is one effective way of moving your opponent around the court. Another is to hit the ball softly onto the front wall. In step 8 you will learn the technique for the drop shot, a softly hit shot aimed just above the tin so that it drops in the front corner, and the lob shot, a softly hit shot aimed high on the front wall so that it arcs into the back corner.

Drop and Lob Shots

One of the most frustrating experiences for a young, fit, aspiring squash player is to come unstuck against an old, overweight player who maneuvers the younger opponent to all corners of the court using deft drops and high lobs. The drop and lob shots complement each other perfectly because they require similar swings, are hit from similar positions, yet end up in opposite areas of the court. For this reason, this step introduces both shots at the same time. Compare the similarities between the shots and see how they can be used together to negate completely the game of a harder-hitting, quicker opponent.

A drop shot is an attacking shot that you hit softly just above the tin on the front wall so that it dies in the frontcourt. You can play it from any position in the court, although the deeper you are, the greater the chance of making an error. Well-executed drop shots often win rallies

outright, although your goal should only be to stretch your opponent forward to the front of the court.

The lob shot—a high, soft shot hit over your opponent's head that drops into the back corner—is generally a defensive shot that you use when you're stretched at the front of the court. Hitting the ball high not only gives your opponent a difficult return, either a high volley or a shot out of the back corner, but also gives you time to recover into position. You can also use the lob to slow the pace of the game. This is a good tactic to use if you're losing and need to disrupt your opponent's rhythm. You can also use the lob as an attacking shot. When you have time at the front of the court, set up as if you're going to play a drop. This will draw your opponent forward, and you can then lob the ball over your incoming opponent's head.

DROP SHOT

At the top level the drop shot is the main weapon used to win rallies. Use the drop either as the winning shot after you've forced your opponent to hit a weak shot, or as a way to move your opponent out of position so that you can hit a winner to the open court with the next shot. The advantage of

the shot is that it forces your opponent to hurry into the front corner with little time to play a good shot. Even though a drop shot often will turn out to be a winning shot, you should think of it as a way of working your opponent, always expecting your opponent to retrieve the ball.

The drop shot is particularly effective if you move quickly to the front of the court after an opponent's boast from the back. This forces your opponent to run diagonally across the court. Experienced players learn to read the boast shot and pounce on it with a delicate drop.

You'll know you're hitting poor drop shots if you continually set up your opponent with easy attacking opportunities. If you're forcing your opponent to stretch forward to return your drop, then you're hitting a reasonably successful shot.

Forehand and Backhand Drop Shots

The drop shot is played like a slow drive, with slightly less backswing and very little follow-through. As you prepare for the shot, bend low to help control the racket face as you strike the ball. Lift the racket face up enough on the backswing to make it look as if you are about to hit a drive. Step across on your front foot (figures 8.1a and 8.2a).

Make sure the racket face is open as you strike the ball so that you slice the shot (figures 8.1b and 8.2b). This will help the ball die after it hits the front wall. Avoid using too much wrist to slice the ball because this often leads to mis-hitting the shot. It's best to keep the wrist firm and push through the ball on impact.

Limit your follow-through and try to push off your front foot quickly so that you can recover to a position to cover your opponent's shot (figures 8.1c and 8.2c). The timing of your step into the shot is important. Try to step and swing at almost the same time so that you can get your momentum into the shot.

| **Figure 8.1** | **Forehand Drop Shot** |

PREPARATION

1. Use short backswing
2. Keep racket face up
3. Bend elbow
4. Step across on front foot
5. Bend knees

a

b

c

EXECUTION

1. Keep racket face open
2. Keep wrist firm
3. Push through ball

FOLLOW-THROUGH

1. Use short follow-through
2. Keep back foot still
3. Push off front foot

Misstep
Your drop shots hit the side wall before the front wall.

Correction
Keep your wrist firm, give yourself plenty of room to swing, and make sure you hit the ball approximately level with your leading foot.

Figure 8.2   Backhand Drop Shot

PREPARATION

1. Use short backswing
2. Hold racket face by back of neck
3. Keep elbow close to body
4. Point elbow down
5. Step across on front foot
6. Bend knees

a

EXECUTION

1. Keep racket face open
2. Keep wrist firm
3. Push through ball

b

FOLLOW-THROUGH

1. Use short follow-through
2. Keep back foot still
3. Push off front foot

c

Misstep
Your drop shots hit too hard or too high on the front wall.

Correction
Keep your wrist firm and use a shorter swing. Don't follow through too much.

Always keep in mind that the drop shot is a way of working your opponent to the front of the court. You shouldn't hit this shot so high that you set up your opponent for a winner or so low that you risk hitting the tin. Also, if you can angle the shot toward the nick, or if you can keep the ball close to the side wall, you'll add to your opponent's difficulties.

 Misstep
Your drop shots hit the tin.

Correction
Keep the racket face open and push through the ball. Aim higher on the front wall to give yourself more room for error.

Forehand Drop Shot With Dynamic Movement

If you are under pressure at the front of the court on the forehand side, use dynamic rather than traditional movement. At full stretch a forehand drop can still be a very effective shot. Lead into the front corner with your back foot (figure 8.3a). As you stretch toward the ball, cock your wrist so that your racket face is up. Keep your wrist firm and your racket face open as you push through the ball (figure 8.3b). Push quickly back to the middle of court to prepare yourself for the next shot.

Figure 8.3   **Forehand Drop Shot With Dynamic Movement**

a

b

PREPARATION

1. Stretch forward on back foot
2. Use short backswing
3. Cock wrist

EXECUTION

1. Keep racket face open
2. Keep wrist firm
3. Push through ball

Misstep
Your drop shot lacks control.

Correction
Attempt a drop only when you have time to set up for the shot. Make sure that you keep your body still as you swing.

Drop Shot Drill 1. *Hand Feed for Drops*

Stand about 10 feet (3 m) from the front wall. Throw the ball against the side wall. After it bounces, hit a straight drop (figure 8.4). Aim your shot just above the tin and close to the side wall. Place a target on the floor about 3 feet (1 m) from the front wall and against the side wall. Try to make your shots bounce on the target. Hit 10 forehand drops and 10 backhand drops.

Figure 8.4 Hand feed for drops.

To Increase Difficulty

- Move the target closer to the front wall.
- Stand farther from the front wall.
- Throw the ball against the front wall, run forward, and hit a drop shot.

To Decrease Difficulty

- Make the target larger.

Success Check

- Step and swing almost simultaneously.
- Keep your wrist firm.
- Keep the racket face open.

Score Your Success

8 to 10 forehand drops that hit the target = 5 points

6 or 7 forehand drops that hit the target = 3 points

4 or 5 forehand drops that hit the target = 1 point

8 to 10 backhand drops that hit the target = 5 points

6 or 7 backhand drops that hit the target = 3 points

4 or 5 backhand drops that hit the target = 1 point

Your score ___

Drop Shot Drill 2. *Racket Feed for Drops*

Stand on the T. Feed the ball across your body so that it hits the front wall and then the side wall. Turn your body and hit a straight drop. Think about angling your shot so that the ball hits the front wall and then hits the floor close to the side-wall nick. Set a target on the floor against the side wall, 3 feet (1 m) from the front wall. Hit 10 forehand drops and 10 backhand drops.

To Increase Difficulty

- Hit crosscourt drops instead of straight drops.
- Feed a high boast and then run forward to hit a straight drop.

To Decrease Difficulty

- Make the target larger.

Success Check

- Step across with your front foot.
- Use a short backswing.
- Slice the ball.

Score Your Success

5 to 10 forehand drops that hit the target = 5 points

3 or 4 forehand drops that hit the target = 3 points

1 or 2 forehand drops that hit the target = 1 point

5 to 10 backhand drops that hit the target = 5 points

3 or 4 backhand drops that hit the target = 3 points

1 or 2 backhand drops that hit the target = 1 point

Your score ____

Drop Shot Drill 3. *Backcourt Drops*

Stand in the back corner and over hit a drive that bounces off the back wall. Hit a drop shot toward a target about 5 feet (1.5 m) from the front wall against the side wall (figure 8.5). Use a little more follow-through to make sure you hit the ball with enough power to reach the front wall above the tin. Give yourself some room for error on the front wall, but keep the ball close to the side wall. You need plenty of slice to make the ball die quickly after hitting the front wall, so make sure that your racket face is open. Hit 10 forehand drops and 10 backhand drops.

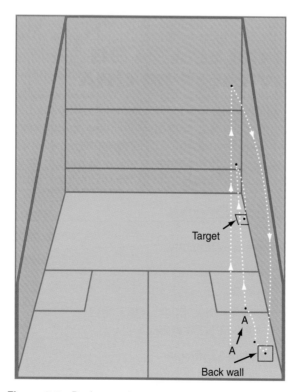

Figure 8.5 Backcourt drops.

To Increase Difficulty

- Move the target closer to the front wall.
- Vary the pace of your drop shots.
- Attempt crosscourt drops instead of straight drop shots.
- Play overhit crosscourt drives; then turn your body and hit a straight drop on the opposite side.

To Decrease Difficulty

- Make the target larger.
- Move the target farther from the front wall.
- Hit your overhit drives farther from the side wall.

Success Check

- Aim higher on the front wall.
- Slice the ball.
- Use a little more follow-through.

Score Your Success

8 to 10 forehand drops that hit the target = 5 points

6 or 7 forehand drops that hit the target = 3 points

4 or 5 forehand drops that hit the target = 1 point

8 to 10 backhand drops that hit the target = 5 points

6 or 7 backhand drops that hit the target = 3 points

4 or 5 backhand drops that hit the target = 1 point

Your score ____

Drop Shot Drill 4. *Drops From a Partner's Feed*

Have a partner stand in the frontcourt about 6 feet (1.8 m) from both the front wall and the side wall. Have your partner feed a straight shot that bounces about halfway between the front wall and the short line. Move forward from the T, hit a straight drop, and then push back to the T. Mark a line on the floor about 3 feet (1 m) from the front wall. Try to hit all your drop shots so that they bounce in front of this line close to the side wall. Your partner should feed continuously rather than stop after each drop shot. Hit 10 forehand drops and 10 backhand drops.

To Increase Difficulty

- Have your partner alternately feed a shot that bounces between the front wall and the short line and a shot that bounces in the service box.
- Have your partner mix up the feeds to work you up and down the length of the court.

To Decrease Difficulty

- Mark the line farther from the front wall.
- Have your partner stop after each drop so that you have more time to prepare for the next feed.

Success Check

- Prepare your racket early.
- Step across with your front foot.
- Bend your knees.

Score Your Success

8 to 10 forehand drops that bounce in front of the line = 5 points

6 or 7 forehand drops that bounce in front of the line = 3 points

4 or 5 forehand drops that bounce in front of the line = 1 point

8 to 10 backhand drops that bounce in front of the line = 5 points

6 or 7 backhand drops that bounce in front of the line = 3 points

4 or 5 backhand drops that bounce in front of the line = 1 point

Your score ____

Drop Shot Drill 5. *Pressure Drops*

Have a partner stand close to the side wall, about 5 feet (1.5 m) from the front wall. Your partner should either hand feed or racket feed the ball so that it bounces about 2 feet (0.6 m) from the front wall. Move forward from the T, hit a drop shot (figure 8.6), and then backpedal to the T. This drill should work you hard for a short period. Your partner's feeds should force you to move quickly and to stretch forward with your front foot to reach the ball before it bounces twice. You'll need only a very short swing, just enough to push the ball onto the front wall. Backpedal quickly after the shot, and make sure you return behind the short line. Hit 15 forehand drop shots and 15 backhand drop shots.

To Decrease Difficulty

- Have your partner feed higher on the front wall to give your more time to get to the ball.

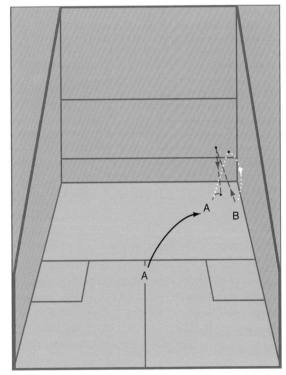

Figure 8.6 Pressure drops.

Success Check

- Stretch your front foot forward.
- Keep your wrist firm.
- Use a short push with the racket face.

Score Your Success

12 to 15 forehand drops that hit above the tin = 5 points

10 or 11 forehand drops that hit above the tin = 3 points

8 or 9 forehand drops that hit above the tin = 1 point

12 to 15 backhand drops that hit above the tin = 5 points

10 or 11 backhand drops that hit above the tin = 3 points

8 or 9 backhand drops that hit above the tin = 1 point

Your score ___

Drop Shot Drill 6. *Drive Your Drops*

This drill forces you to shorten your follow-through because if you don't, you won't have enough time to prepare the racket for the drive. Have a partner stand in the back corner and feed a straight shot to the frontcourt. From the T, move forward, hit a straight drop, and then hit a straight drive back to your partner off your drop shot. Aim to hit the drop shot low enough so that after the drop you can drag your back foot to your front foot. Then step forward again on the front foot for the drive. Hit 10 forehand drop shots and drives and 10 backhand drop shots and drives.

To Increase Difficulty

- Have your partner hit boasts. Move from side to side, hitting straight drops followed by straight drives.
- Have your partner hit a boast. Hit a crosscourt drop, and then move across to hit a straight drive.

Success Check

- Prepare your racket quickly.
- Keep your body still when driving.
- Stay low.

Score Your Success

8 to 10 successful forehand drop shots and drives = 5 points

6 or 7 successful forehand drop shots and drives = 3 points

4 or 5 successful forehand drop shots and drives = 1 point

8 to 10 successful backhand drop shots and drives = 5 points

6 or 7 successful backhand drop shots and drives = 3 points

4 or 5 successful backhand drop shots and drives = 1 point

Your score ___

Drop Shot Drill 7. *Boast and Drop Pressure Drill*

Have a partner stand in the front corner and hit a crosscourt drive. Stand at the back of the court and hit a boast (figure 8.7a). Your partner then hits a straight drop. Run forward and hit a straight drop off the drop (figure 8.7b). Your partner then hits another crosscourt, taking you to the back of the court to boast again. As you move forward,

think about moving through the T. Always move between your partner and the side wall. Once you hit the drop shot, push back to the T, again staying between your partner and the side wall. Then turn and move back for the boast. Hit 15 forehand drop shots and 15 backhand drop shots. Keep shots above the tin.

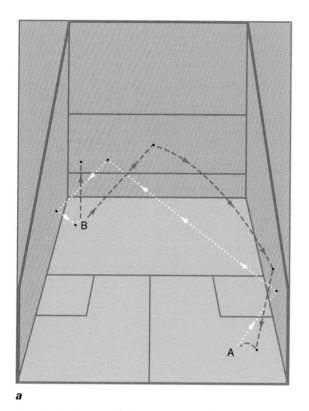
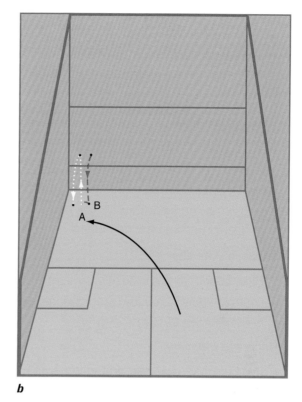

a   b

Figure 8.7 Boast and drop pressure drill: *(a)* hit a boast from the backcourt; *(b)* move forward to hit a straight drop off the partner's drop shot.

To Increase Difficulty

- Have your partner hit either straight or cross-court drops. You must hit a straight drop to whichever front corner the ball goes to.
- Have your partner randomly hit straight drops and crosscourt drives. You hit boasts off the crosscourt drives and straight drops off the drops.

To Decrease Difficulty

- Have your partner hit higher drops to give you more time to get to the ball.

Success Check

- Step forward with your front foot.
- Prepare your racket early.
- Use a short follow-through.

Score Your Success

12 to 15 forehand drops that hit above the tin = 5 points

10 or 11 forehand drops that hit above the tin = 3 points

8 or 9 forehand drops that hit above the tin = 1 point

12 to 15 backhand drops that hit above the tin = 5 points

10 or 11 backhand drops that hit above the tin = 3 points

8 or 9 backhand drops that hit above the tin = 1 point

Your score ____

Drop Shot Drill 8. *Boast-Drop-Drive*

Your partner starts by hitting a boast from the back corner. Stand in the front corner and hit a straight drop. After hitting the drop, move back to the middle, giving your partner room to move between you and the side wall. Your partner then runs forward and hits a straight drive off your drop. You must then run back and hit a boast. Your partner hits a straight drop, and you run forward and hit a straight drive. Remember to go through the T when moving forward after the boast. See how long you can keep the drill going.

To Increase Difficulty

- Hit crosscourt drops instead of straight drops.
- Let the person hitting the drop choose to hit either straight or crosscourt.

To Decrease Difficulty

- Instead of keeping the drill going continuously, stop after you've each hit a boast, a drop, and a drive so that you can catch your breath. Repeat.

Success Check

- Move through the T.
- Move quickly and smoothly.
- Keep your body still when you swing.

Score Your Success

Keep the drill going for more than 5 minutes = 10 points

Keep the drill going for 3 to 5 minutes = 5 points

Keep the drill going for less than 3 minutes = 1 point

Your score ___

LOB SHOT

Use the lob shot primarily as a defensive shot. Normally, when your opponent's good shot has forced you to fully stretch at the front of the court, the lob is the only shot that will keep you in the rally. A straight drive is usually impossible because the ball is so far in front of you. Your opponent will be on the T just waiting for a crosscourt drive to hit to the opposite back corner to make you run the diagonal. A drop is a possibility, but may be difficult to execute well enough to avoid leaving you stranded at the front of the court. The alternative is to lift the ball as high as you can in the hope that it will go over your opponent's head. This will force your opponent to move to the back corner to retrieve it or at least stretch up and hit a difficult high volley. A well-executed lob can often immediately turn a defensive position into an offensive one.

As with the drop shot, it's important to bend down to the ball for the lob shot. On the forehand side, you can use either traditional or dynamic movement, but because the lob is often a way of releasing pressure, you will likely be stretching for the ball, which means more often than not that you will want to use dynamic movement and stretch with your back foot toward the ball (figure 8.8a). On the backhand side, you should stretch forward with your front foot (figure 8.9a). Prepare the racket face early, but use a shorter backswing than you use for the drive.

Get the racket face underneath the ball as you strike it so that you can lift it high onto the front wall (figures 8.8b and 8.9b). A slight flick with the wrist will sometimes provide the lift you need on the shot, but be careful not to use so much wrist that you lose control of the shot.

As you follow through, keep your body still and finish with the racket face up high (figures 8.8c and 8.9c). Once you have finished the shot, push off your front foot and move back to the middle of the court.

Figure 8.8   Forehand Lob Shot

PREPARATION

1. Stretch forward with back foot
2. Use short backswing
3. Cock wrist
4. Keep racket face up
5. Keep elbow bent
6. Bend low

a

EXECUTION

1. Place racket face underneath ball
2. Flick wrist slightly
3. Aim high on front wall

b

FOLLOW-THROUGH

1. Keep body still
2. Finish with racket high
3. Push off back foot

c

Misstep
There is not enough height on your lobs.

Correction
Bend lower to get underneath the ball. Flick your wrist slightly to lift the ball more.

Figure 8.9   Backhand Lob Shot

PREPARATION

1. Stretch forward with front foot
2. Use short backswing
3. Hold racket face behind neck
4. Cock wrist
5. Bend low

a

EXECUTION

1. Place racket face underneath ball
2. Flick wrist slightly
3. Aim high on front wall

b

FOLLOW-THROUGH

1. Keep body still
2. Finish with racket high
3. Push off front foot

c

Misstep
Your lobs lack control.

Correction
Keep your body and feet still as you swing through.

The lob can be hit either straight or crosscourt. Crosscourt lobs usually are easier to hit, particularly if you're stretching forward for the shot. You also have more room for error on a crosscourt lob. If you hit straight, the ball must stay close to the side wall or you may risk giving up a penalty point by hitting it back to yourself.

Aim the crosscourt lob to hit the side wall close to the back of the service box so that it bounces close to the back wall. Be careful about hitting out of court. It's better to hit high on the front wall and down the middle of the court than risk hitting out of court on the side wall or not getting the ball over your opponent's head.

Misstep
The ball goes out of court when you hit a lob.

Correction
Keep your wrist a little firmer as you swing. Don't aim as far across the front wall when hitting a crosscourt lob.

As with the drop shot, a poor lob will set up your opponent with an easy attacking opportunity. Your goal is to force your opponent to hit from a position in which he is stretched up high.

Lob Shot Drill 1. *Hand Feed for Lobs*

Stand in the middle of the court about 10 feet (3 m) from the front wall. Throw the ball into the front corner so it hits the front wall and then the side wall. Run forward and hit a straight lob into the back corner. Step forward with your front foot and bend low so that you can get your racket face underneath the ball. Lift the ball high onto the front wall so that the ball arcs into the back corner. Aim for the ball to bounce between the back of the service box and the back wall no farther from the side wall than the width of the service box. Hit 10 forehand lobs and 10 backhand lobs.

To Increase Difficulty

- Aim for a target on the floor about 3 feet (1 m) from the back wall, against the side wall.
- Hit crosscourt lobs, instead of straight lobs, toward the opposite back corner.

To Decrease Difficulty

- Stand about 6 feet (1.8 m) from the side wall, throw the ball against the side wall, and then step across and hit either straight or crosscourt lobs.

Success Check

- Keep the racket face open.
- Bend low.
- Aim high on the front wall.

Score Your Success

8 to 10 forehand lobs that bounce behind the service box = 5 points

6 or 7 forehand lobs that bounce behind the service box = 3 points

4 or 5 forehand lobs that bounce behind the service box = 1 point

8 to 10 backhand lobs that bounce behind the service box = 5 points

6 or 7 backhand lobs that bounce behind the service box = 3 points

4 or 5 backhand lobs that bounce behind the service box = 1 point

Your score ___

Lob Shot Drill 2. *Racket Feed for Lobs*

Stand on the T. Feed a high boast, and then run forward and hit alternating straight and crosscourt lobs into the back corners (figure 8.10). Put targets in the back corners. For the straight lob, the target should be about 3 feet (1 m) from the back wall and against the side wall. For the crosscourt lob, the target should also be about 3 feet (1 m) from the back wall but slightly away from the side wall. Your goal on the crosscourt lob

is to make the ball hit the side wall and bounce onto the target. Hit 10 forehand lobs and 10 backhand lobs.

To Increase Difficulty

• Hit your boast lower on the front wall.

To Decrease Difficulty

• Remove the targets and concentrate only on getting some height on your lobs.

Success Check

• Prepare your racket early.
• Use a short backswing.
• Flick your wrist slightly.

Score Your Success

5 to 10 forehand lobs that hit the target = 5 points

3 or 4 forehand lobs that hit the target = 3 points

1 or 2 forehand lobs that hit the target = 1 point

5 to 10 backhand lobs that hit the target = 5 points

3 or 4 backhand lobs that hit the target = 3 points

1 or 2 backhand lobs that hit the target = 1 point

Your score ___

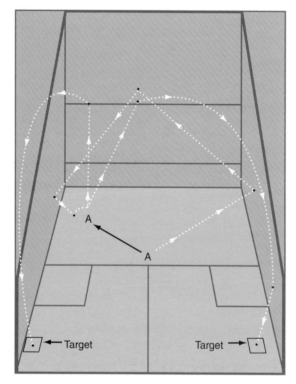

Figure 8.10 Racket feed for lobs.

Lob Shot Drill 3. *Lobs From a Partner's Feed*

Have a partner stand in the back corner and feed a short shot to the frontcourt. Move forward from the T, hit a straight lob, and then push back to the T. As in Lob Shot Drill 2, set a target at the back of the court. Hit 10 forehand lobs and 10 backhand lobs.

To Increase Difficulty

• Have your partner feed boasts for you to hit crosscourt lobs.

To Decrease Difficulty

• Make the target larger.
• Have your partner feed higher on the front wall.

Success Check

• Watch the ball.
• Step across on your front foot.
• Keep the racket face underneath the ball.

5 to 10 forehand lobs that hit the target = 5 points

3 or 4 forehand lobs that hit the target = 3 points

1 or 2 forehand lobs that hit the target = 1 point

5 to 10 backhand lobs that hit the target = 5 points

3 or 4 backhand lobs that hit the target = 3 points

1 or 2 backhand lobs that hit the target = 1 point

Your score ___

Lob Shot Drill 4. *Lob and Boast Routine*

Have a partner stand in the backcourt and move from side to side, alternately hitting forehand and backhand boasts. Stand in the frontcourt and move from side to side, alternately hitting forehand and backhand straight lobs. Try to move to and from the T between shots. If you're getting enough height on your lobs, you should be able to get back to the T in plenty of time for the next shot. See how long you can keep the drill going.

To Increase Difficulty

- Have your partner hit straight drop shots for you to hit crosscourt lobs.
- Have your partner hit straight drop shots for you to alternate between hitting straight and crosscourt lobs.

To Decrease Difficulty

- Have your partner hit the boasts higher on the front wall.

Success Check

- Move forward in a slight J shape.
- Prepare your racket early.
- Keep your body still as you swing.

Keep the drill going for more than 5 minutes = 10 points

Keep the drill going for 3 to 5 minutes = 5 points

Keep the drill going for less than 3 minutes = 1 point

Your score ___

Lob Shot Drill 5. *Back Versus Front Lobs*

Play a conditioned, or modified, game in which your partner can hit any shot that bounces in front of the short line. You must hit either a straight or crosscourt lob. Play the game with point-per-rally scoring to 11 points, with you serving each time. Play three games.

To Increase Difficulty

- Change the rules so that you must hit either all straight lobs or all crosscourt lobs.

To Decrease Difficulty:

- Change the rules so that your opponent must hit either all straight drops or all boasts.

Success Check

- Turn your head to watch the ball in the backcourt.
- Move back to the T after each shot.
- Keep your racket face open.

Win two or three games against your opponent = 5 points

Win one game against your opponent = 3 points

Your score ___

Lob Shot Drill 6.   *Two-Ball Feeds for Lobs*

Two feeders, each with a ball, stand in the back corners and hit short feeds to the front corners. Move from side to side, alternately hitting forehand and backhand straight lobs. Try to watch the feeders as they strike the ball. Concentrate on stepping across on your front foot for each shot. Place a target on the floor in each back corner against the side wall and about 3 feet (1 m) from the back wall. See how many times you can hit the targets in 5 minutes.

To Increase Difficulty

- Have the feeders feed more quickly and lower on the front wall.

To Decrease Difficulty

- Make the targets larger.
- Have the feeders feed more slowly and higher on the front wall.

Success Check

- Watch the ball.
- Bend low.
- Sidestep across the court.

Score Your Success

Hit the target 10 times or more in 5 minutes = 5 points

Hit the target 7 to 9 times in 5 minutes = 3 points

Hit the target 6 times or fewer in 5 minutes = 1 point

Your score ___

SUCCESS SUMMARY
FOR DROP AND LOB SHOTS

If you want to win rallies, you must learn the finer points of the drop shot. If you want to stay in rallies, you must develop a good lob shot. The drop—a softly hit shot that hits the front wall and dies soon after—relies on a shortened backswing with some element of disguise. The lob—a soft shot hit high onto the front wall to arc into the back corner—usually is a defensive shot. Use the lob when you're under pressure to slow the game and move your opponent into the backcourt. Have an observer watch you practice lobs and drop shots and rate your skill using figures 8.1 through 8.3 and figures 8.8 and 8.9.

Before moving on to step 9, Kill Shots, evaluate how you did on the drills in this step. Tally your scores to determine how well you have mastered lob and drop shots. If you scored 110 points or more, you are ready to move on to step 9. If you did not score at least 110 points, practice the drills again until you raise your scores before moving on to step 9.

Drop Shot Drills

1. Hand Feed for Drops   ___ out of 10

2. Racket Feed for Drops   ___ out of 10

3. Backcourt Drops   ___ out of 10

4. Drops From a Partner's Feed   ___ out of 10

5. Pressure Drops   ___ out of 10

6. Drive Your Drops   ___ out of 10

7. Boast and Drop Pressure Drill   ___ out of 10

8. Boast-Drop-Drive   ___ out of 10

Lob Shot Drills

1. Hand Feed for Lobs   ___ out of 10

2. Racket Feed for Lobs   ___ out of 10

3. Lobs From a Partner's Feed   ___ out of 10

4. Lob and Boast Routine   ___ out of 10

5. Back Versus Front Lobs   ___ out of 5

6. Two-Ball Feeds for Lobs   ___ out of 5

Total   ___ **out of 130**

In addition to being able to slow the pace of the ball down with drops and lobs, it is important to be able to end rallies with hard-hit, low shots. In step 9, you will learn how to execute the kill shot. A kill shot is an attacking shot hit with power just above the tin. If hit well, the kill shot rebounds off the front wall into the nick and rolls out along the floor, giving your opponent no opportunity to hit a return.

Kill Shots

Watching a player who can hit an array of kill shots on the squash court can be exhilarating. But it can be disheartening if you are the one facing that player. Such an opponent will dispatch the slightest wayward shot into the nick, leaving you chasing the ball as it rolls along the floor.

Kill shots are hit hard with slice, just above the tin and, if possible, angled toward the nick. Because the shot must be hit low on the front wall, there is little room for error. A shot hit too high will bounce up into the middle of the court, giving your opponent the advantage. A shot hit too low will hit the tin. Therefore, you should attempt a kill shot only when you have drawn a loose shot from your opponent and have the ball set up nicely for you. Practice the kill shot before attempting it in match situations. You must feel confident about playing the kill shot, or it will end up turning good opportunities into points lost.

In a tight match often the player who comes out on top is the one who is prepared to step up and attack. You can do this by volleying more. Another way of attacking your opponent, when left with the right opportunity, is attempting to kill the ball—that is, hit it so that it is unreturnable.

If you don't develop a kill shot, you'll often find yourself having difficulty finishing a rally, even if your opponent is hitting loose shots. This is particularly true if you're playing on a hot court and the ball is bouncing up more than usual. In these conditions it can be difficult to put away your opponent with drops, good-length drives, and lobs. If you can't hit a kill shot, you'll win only by wearing down your opponent, which can often take a great physical toll on you as well.

You can tell when you are hitting good kill shots because your opponent won't be able to return them. Remember, you should attempt kill shots only when you have worked a good opening.

STRAIGHT KILL

Play the straight kill from anywhere in the court as long as the ball isn't too close to the side or back walls. You should never attempt the straight kill if you feel at all rushed. Generally, the farther back in the court you are, the harder the shot is.

Some players use the kill effectively off overhit shots that have bounced off the side and back toward the middle of the court.

As with all shots, make sure you have the racket prepared early. Step across on your front foot, turning your front shoulder toward the side wall (figures 9.1*a* and 9.2*a*). Have your racket face open, and use a high backswing.

Strike the ball earlier than you do during a drive shot—that is, closer to the top of the bounce. As you swing, think about trying to hit down the back of the ball (figures 9.1*b* and 9.2*b*). By using an open racket face, you should be able to hit with plenty of slice. What you need to develop as you practice this shot is the right combination of racket-head speed and control. Your wrist and grip should be relaxed so that you can whip the racket face through with plenty of pace. You must not lose control of the racket face, however, or the open face will cause you to mis-hit the shot.

As you follow through, begin to grip the racket more tightly (figures 9.1*c* and 9.2*c*). This will enable you to control the swing right through the completion of the shot.

Figure 9.1   Forehand Straight Kill Shot

PREPARATION
1. Step across on front foot
2. Turn front shoulder to side wall
3. Use high backswing
4. Cock wrist
5. Bend elbow
6. Loosen grip
7. Keep racket face open

a

EXECUTION
1. Hit at top of bounce
2. Hit down back of ball
3. Keep body still

b

FOLLOW-THROUGH
1. Control racket face
2. Grip racket more tightly

c

Misstep
Your kill shots hit the tin.

Correction
Make sure that you hit the shot at the top of the bounce. If you let the ball drop as far as you would for a drive, it will be difficult to hit down on the ball and keep the ball from hitting the tin.

Figure 9.2 | Backhand Straight Kill Shot

PREPARATION

1. Step across on front foot
2. Turn front shoulder to side wall
3. Use high backswing
4. Hold racket face by back of neck
5. Loosen grip
6. Keep racket face open

a

EXECUTION

1. Hit at top of bounce
2. Hit down back of ball
3. Keep body still

b

FOLLOW-THROUGH

1. Control racket face
2. Grip racket more tightly

c

Aim the ball just above the tin, and angle it toward the nick. Always attempt to hit the nick because this is what will make the shot unreturnable. Some players think that hitting the nick is just luck. This isn't true. The more you practice, the more you'll develop the feel for the sort of angle you need to hit the nick.

FOREHAND STRAIGHT KILL WITH DYNAMIC MOVEMENT

When the ball is coming at you fast on the forehand side, it is typically easier and more efficient to use dynamic movement and hit your kill shot off the back foot. It is also good to hit off the back foot if you are stepping back slightly to the ball. Attempting a kill shot from this position can be a low-percentage shot, so try it only if you are well balanced and feel confident with your positioning and swing.

As you step across to the ball, turn your shoulders slightly toward the side wall (figure 9.3a). Prepare your racket early, keep your racket face open, and use a high backswing. Strike the ball at the top of the bounce, and think about hitting down the back of the ball (figure 9.3b). As soon as you have finished the follow-through, push back to the T.

Figure 9.3   Forehand Straight Kill With Dynamic Movement

a

b

PREPARATION

1. Step across on back foot
2. Turn front shoulder slightly toward side wall
3. Use high backswing
4. Loosen grip
5. Keep racket face open

EXECUTION

1. Hit ball at top of bounce
2. Hit down back of ball
3. Keep body still

CROSSCOURT KILL

Usually, you should attempt the crosscourt kill (figure 9.4) only in the front half of the court. The crosscourt kill is easier to hit than the straight kill, but beware; if your opponent can get the ball back, you'll find yourself badly out of position.

Hit the ball out in front of you. Take the ball early, hitting it close to the top of the bounce so that you can hit the ball down toward the nick.

Figure 9.4   Crosscourt Kill

a

b

PREPARATION

1. Prepare racket early
2. Bend knees
3. Keep racket face open

EXECUTION

1. Hit ball out in front
2. Hit ball at top of bounce
3. Hit with slice
4. Control swing
5. Aim to hit nick or for ball to bounce twice before reaching side wall

Misstep
You have no control over your kill shots.

Correction
Keep your body still as you swing. Also, even though you are swinging through quickly, try to keep your racket face under control.

You can play the crosscourt kill in two ways. You can aim the ball straight for the side-wall nick after hitting the front wall, or you can aim it to bounce twice before reaching the side wall. Players more frequently go for the nick. Make sure, though, that if you miss the nick, you at least hit the side wall first. This will keep the ball lower, making the return more difficult.

Usually, players attempt the second option when up close to the front wall. You can increase the effectiveness by holding the shot and trying to send your opponent the wrong way. With both shots, control and slice are more important than just hitting the ball hard.

VOLLEY KILL

Killing the ball on the volley is often easier because you can take the ball from higher in the air than you can after it bounces. You can hit volley kills from anywhere on the court, but again, the farther back in the court you are, the greater the risk. You can hit a volley kill straight or crosscourt.

Often, players use the straight volley kill to intercept an opponent's crosscourt. This is especially effective on a crosscourt from the back because you will then send your opponent diagonally to the opposite corner. The straight volley kill is often hit as a reflex shot off an opponent's loose drive, so quick preparation is essential to have any hope of consistently hitting a winner. The faster the ball comes at you, the shorter the required swing. Off an opponent's hard shot, take a short backswing (figure 9.5a) and punch the ball into the front corner. Keep the wrist firm and the racket face open so that you slice the ball (figure 9.5b). If your opponent's shot has less pace, you'll need a larger backswing and a faster swing-through to generate some pace on the shot. If you have to reach up for the shot, you'll need to loosen your wrist slightly so that you can bring the ball down. Yet you must still try to control the racket face as you swing through.

Figure 9.5   Volley Kill

PREPARATION

1. Prepare racket early
2. Use short, punchy swing
3. Keep racket face open

EXECUTION

1. Hit with slice
2. Control racket face

Misstep
Your kill shots bounce up too much.

Correction
Hit your shot with more slice so that the ball dies more quickly after hitting the front wall. Open your racket face more, and think about cutting down the back of the ball.

The crosscourt volley kill is usually played from head height or above, usually off a loose shot in the midcourt area. The crosscourt volley kill can be a particularly effective way to attack a bad serve. Again, hit the shot with plenty of slice. The wrist needs to be slightly looser than it is for most other shots so that you can whip the racket face through quickly. Aim to hit the front wall and then the side-wall nick. If it misses the nick, the ball should at least hit the side wall before the floor so that it doesn't bounce up too much.

Kill Shot Drill 1. *Racket Feed for Kills*

Stand on the T. Hit a soft, high feed that bounces about halfway between the front wall and the short line. Step forward and hit a straight kill. Your feed should be at least a couple of feet away from the side wall so that you can try to angle the ball toward the nick. Remember to hit the ball at the top of the bounce and to hit with plenty of slice. Hit 10 forehand kills and 10 backhand kills.

To Increase Difficulty

- Stand farther back and hit kills from feeds that bounce in the service box.
- Feed the ball higher and hit straight volley kills.

Success Check

- Prepare the racket early and high.
- Hit down the back of the ball.
- Swing through quickly.

Score Your Success

5 to 10 forehand kills that hit the nick = 5 points

3 or 4 forehand kills that hit the nick = 3 points

1 or 2 forehand kills that hit the nick = 1 point

5 to 10 backhand kills that hit the nick = 5 points

3 or 4 backhand kills that hit the nick = 3 points

1 or 2 backhand kills that hit the nick = 1 point

Your score ___

Kill Shot Drill 2. *Crosscourt Kills*

Stand on the forehand side of the court about 8 feet (2.4 m) from the front wall and about 5 feet (1.5 m) from the side wall. Turn your body so that you face the opposite side wall. Hit a backhand shot high on the opposite side wall so that it rebounds off the front wall and bounces between you and the front wall. Turn your body toward the front wall, and prepare your racket for a forehand. As the ball reaches the top of the bounce, hit a forehand crosscourt kill. Aim your shot to hit the nick. If the ball doesn't roll out of the nick, turn and try to feed again with the backhand without stopping. Repeat on the opposite side for backhand crosscourt kills. Hit 10 forehand kills and 10 backhand kills.

To Increase Difficulty

- Hit the feeds harder and lower.

Success Check

- Keep your wrist loose.
- Angle the ball toward the nick.
- Bend your knees as you swing.

Score Your Success

5 to 10 forehand kills that hit the nick = 5 points

3 or 4 forehand kills that hit the nick = 3 points

1 or 2 forehand kills that hit the nick = 1 point

5 to 10 backhand kills that hit the nick = 5 points

3 or 4 backhand kills that hit the nick = 3 points

1 or 2 backhand kills that hit the nick = 1 point

Your score ___

Kill Shot Drill 3. *Crosscourt Volley Kills*

Stand on the T. Feed the ball with a backhand across your body so that it hits the front wall close to the side wall and then rebounds off the side wall to you in the middle (figure 9.6). Hit a forehand crosscourt volley kill. Make sure that you hit your kill shot far enough across the court so that if the ball doesn't hit the nick, it will at least hit the side wall before hitting the floor. If

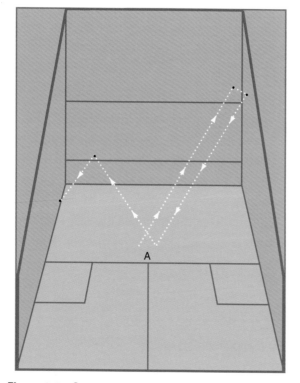

Figure 9.6 Crosscourt volley kills.

the ball bounces up enough, turn and feed the ball again without stopping. (However, your goal is to make the ball irretrievable.) After practicing forehand kills, hit forehand feeds for backhand crosscourt volley kills. Hit 10 forehand kills and 10 backhand kills.

To Increase Difficulty

- Hit the feeds harder to force yourself to prepare the racket more quickly.

To Decrease Difficulty

- Feed the ball more softly, let it bounce, and then hit a crosscourt kill.

Success Check

- Hit with plenty of slice.
- Hit the ball in front of you.
- Keep your feet still as you swing.

Score Your Success

5 to 10 forehand kills that hit the nick = 5 points

3 or 4 forehand kills that hit the nick = 3 points

1 or 2 forehand kills that hit the nick = 1 point

5 to 10 backhand kills that hit the nick = 5 points

3 or 4 backhand kills that hit the nick = 3 points

1 or 2 backhand kills that hit the nick = 1 point

Your score ____

Kill Shot Drill 4. *Kill Shots From a Partner's Feed*

Have a partner stand in the service box and feed the ball straight so that it bounces about halfway between the front wall and the short line (figure 9.7). Move forward from the T and hit a straight kill shot. Try to hit your shot so that your partner can't return it. If the feed is close to the side wall, hit the ball tight to the side wall. If the feed is away from the side wall, angle your shot toward the nick. Hit 10 forehand kills and 10 backhand kills.

To Increase Difficulty

- Hit crosscourt kills instead of straight kills.
- Have your partner feed higher on the front wall for you to hit volley kills.

Success Check

- Step across on your front foot.
- Turn your front shoulder toward the side wall.
- Hit the ball at the top of the bounce.

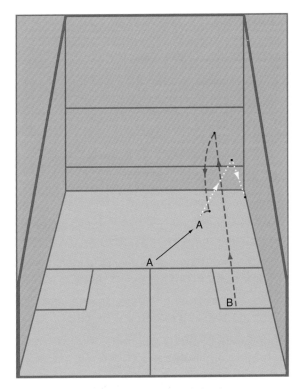

Figure 9.7 Kill shots from a partner's feed.

Score Your Success

5 to 10 unreturnable forehand kills = 5 points

3 or 4 unreturnable forehand kills = 3 points

1 or 2 unreturnable forehand kills = 1 point

5 to 10 unreturnable backhand kills = 5 points

3 or 4 unreturnable backhand kills = 3 points

1 or 2 unreturnable backhand kills = 1 point

Your score ___

Kill Shot Drill 5. *Frontcourt Game*

Play a game with your opponent in which all shots must bounce in front of the short line. Begin each rally by serving from in front of the service box. The serve can be hit anywhere in the frontcourt but not for a winner. If you do win the rally off the serve, replay the point. Play point-per-rally scoring to 11 points. Encourage kill shots by awarding 2 points for any kill shot that hits the nick and is unreturnable. Play three games.

To Increase Difficulty

• Draw a line closer to the front wall, and change the rules so that the ball can't bounce beyond that line.

To Decrease Difficulty

• Play with the same rules except that your opponent can hit only straight shots.

Success Check

• Keep your racket face up.

• Aim for the nick whenever possible.

• Slice all your shots.

Score Your Success

Win two or three games against your opponent = 5 points

Win one game against your opponent = 3 points

Your score ___

Kill Shot Drill 6. *Cutting Off Crosscourt Drives*

You and a partner stand on the short line on opposite sides of the court. Your partner hits a crosscourt drive, which you cut off with a straight volley kill. After your kill shot, step forward and hit a crosscourt back so your partner can hit a straight volley kill. Don't worry if the ball bounces more than once before you can hit the crosscourt shot back to your partner. In fact, it's preferable that your volley kill be too good for you to reach before the second bounce. See how long you can keep the drill going while hitting forehand volley kills. Then repeat the drill using backhand volley kills.

To Increase Difficulty

• Hit crosscourt drives with more pace.

To Decrease Difficulty

• Hit crosscourt drives with less pace.

Success Check

• Don't back up from the short line.
• Prepare your racket early.
• Use a short swing.

Score Your Success

Keep the drill going with forehand volley kills for more than 3 minutes = 5 points

Keep the drill going with forehand volley kills for 2 to 3 minutes = 3 points

Keep the drill going with forehand volley kills for less than 2 minutes = 1 point

Keep the drill going with backhand volley kills for more than 3 minutes = 5 points

Keep the drill going with backhand volley kills for 2 to 3 minutes = 3 points

Keep the drill going with backhand volley kills for less than 2 minutes = 1 point

Your score ___

Kill Shot Drill 7. *Two-Ball Feeds for Kills*

Two feeders stand in the service boxes and alternately feed you straight shots that bounce about halfway between the front wall and the short line. Move from side to side, hitting straight kill shots. Have your partners count how many of your shots they couldn't get their racket face on before the ball bounced twice. Perform the drill for 3 minutes.

To Increase Difficulty

• Have feeders feed faster, forcing you to move more quickly.

To Decrease Difficulty

• Have feeders feed only when you have turned and are ready for the shot.

Success Check

• Sidestep across the court.
• Prepare your racket early.
• Hit down on the ball.

Score Your Success

20 or more unreturnable shots in 3 minutes = 10 points

10 to 19 unreturnable shots in 3 minutes = 5 points

9 or fewer unreturnable shots in 3 minutes = 1 point

Your score ___

SUCCESS SUMMARY FOR KILL SHOTS

Without a well-developed kill shot, you'll struggle to win rallies off an opponent's loose shots. The only way you'll be able to win is by wearing down your opponent. With the kill shot you can take advantage of a loose ball by hitting it low onto the front wall so that it dies in the nick.

Never attempt a kill when you feel rushed or when cramped in the back corners. This shot requires much practice before you use it in a match situation; you have limited room for error.

Have a partner watch you practice to check your stroke against figures 9.1 through 9.5.

Before moving on to step 10, Disguise and Deception, evaluate how you did on the drills in this step. Tally your scores to determine how well you have mastered kill shots. If you scored 50 points or more, you are ready to move on to step 10. If you did not score at least 50 points, practice the drills again until you raise your scores before moving on to step 10.

Kill Shot Drills

1. Racket Feed for Kills	___ out of 10
2. Crosscourt Kills	___ out of 10
3. Crosscourt Volley Kills	___ out of 10
4. Kill Shots From a Partner's Feed	___ out of 10
5. Frontcourt Game	___ out of 5
6. Cutting Off Crosscourt Drives	___ out of 10
7. Two-Ball Feeds for Kills	___ out of 10
Total	___ *out of 65*

At this point you should have a good grasp of all the basic squash shots. Even if you can execute all these shots reasonably well, you will still find yourself in difficulties if your opponent can easily read which shot you are about to hit. Step 10 will help you be less predictable by intro-ducing the concepts of disguise and deception. Disguise is about setting up in such a way that your opponent cannot tell which shot you are about to play. Deception is about making it look as though you are going to play a particular shot, but then actually hitting something different.

STEP

10

Disguise and Deception

In previous steps, we looked at two ways to apply pressure to your opponent—the volley and the kill. We'll now consider a third way—using disguise and deception to send your opponent the wrong way (i.e., to wrong-foot your opponent) or at least keep your opponent guessing about where you're going to hit the ball, right up to the time you strike it.

Many players are under the misconception that disguise and deception are the same. This isn't true. *Disguise* is setting up for a shot in such a way that your opponent can't tell which shot you're about to play. *Deception* is setting up so that it looks as though you're going to play a particular shot, but you actually play another. When used effectively, disguise and deception

can unsettle your opponent because she is never sure which way to move.

When played well, deception can be devastating because it makes it difficult for your opponent to keep from moving before you strike the ball. Hitting with deception, however, requires that you use your wrist, and you'll often have to hit from an awkward body position. Thus, you risk hitting a weak shot. Bring deception into your game slowly, experimenting with various racket preparations and body positions to see what works. Don't overdo it, though. Subtle changes often completely fool your opponent, but exaggerated changes immediately signal your opponent to watch the ball, not your body or racket.

DISGUISE

As you begin to play at higher levels, you'll find that your opponents are skillful at reading where you're going to hit the ball. You need to develop disguise to stop them from anticipating your shot and pouncing on the ball before you've had a chance to recover. If you disguise your shots, your opponent must wait on the T until you've hit the ball or risk moving in the wrong direction, handing you an easy point.

Top-level players use disguise constantly by preparing early and in a similar way for all shots. When advanced players have time, you'll find it almost impossible to read what shot they're going to play until they play it. Remember these points when trying to increase the disguise on your shots:

- **Hold the shot**. This means waiting until the last possible moment to strike the ball. Holding your shots can cause your opponent to commit to moving in a particular direction before he is sure where the ball is going.

- **Prepare the racket early.** As you begin to practice your shots in game situations, concentrate on preparing the racket early. This will help you hold your shots.
- **Be decisive.** Even though you hope your opponent has no idea where the ball is

going, be sure you know where you want to hit it. Any indecision on your part could cause you to mis-hit the shot and lose the rally from a strong position.

Also realize that because all shots in squash are variations of the basic swing, you'll inherently build disguise into your game as your stroke production improves. So work constantly on the basics of your technique.

Misstep
You mis-hit your shot when you try to disguise it.

Correction
Try to relax more as you hit your shots and avoid trying so hard to disguise your shot, which leads to indecision or to not properly executing the swing.

DECEPTION

In the middle of a close match, winning a point can be like climbing a mountain. If you and your opponent are evenly matched, it helps to have some tricks up your sleeve to pull out during crucial rallies. Deception will give you this edge because, like the kill shot, it often leads to outright winners or at least puts your opponent well out of position. Deception has an advantage over the kill shot because even if you don't hit the shot perfectly (a frequent occurrence during tight matches), it's less likely to hit the tin.

Bring deception into your match play slowly, improvising now and again with a variety of body movements and hitting the ball from various positions in relation to your body. Use it sparingly, always keeping in mind that if you try to deceive your opponent too many times in the same way, she will catch on and start reading what you're going to do.

Attempt deception in matches only after you practice and become comfortable with the shots. First, experiment on your own with various racket and body positions. At this stage you shouldn't hesitate to try anything. In game situations, however, you should limit yourself to hitting deceptive shots that you feel comfortable with. The following sections

offer four examples of deception shots used in match play

Example 1

At the front of the court, set up for a drop shot with a short backswing and the racket face low (figure 10.1a). Hold the shot as long as possible. As your opponent starts to move forward, use your wrist to hit a hard crosscourt drive (figure 10.1b).

Example 2

Set up with your body facing the front wall instead of the side wall, making it look as if you're going to hit crosscourt (figure 10.2a). Instead, punch the ball as hard as you can straight down the wall (figure 10.2b). Turning your head toward the middle of the court as you strike the ball (the no-look shot) will add to the deception.

Example 3

In the back corner, turn your body so that you face the back wall as if you're going to play a boast (figure 10.3a). Wait for the ball to come as far off the back wall as possible and drive the ball straight down the wall (figure 10.3b). Use a little wrist if necessary.

a   b

Figure 10.1   Preparing for a straight drop *(a)*, and then hitting a crosscourt drive *(b)*.

a   b

Figure 10.2   Preparing for a crosscourt drive *(a)*, and then hitting a straight drive *(b)*.

a   b

Figure 10.3   Preparing for a boast *(a)*, and then hitting a straight drive *(b)*.

Example 4

Set up anywhere in the court for a straight drive with the racket up early and high (figure 10.4a). Wait for the ball to come to your side, or even slightly behind you, to make it seem as if you could only play a straight drive or boast. Then, as you swing through, flick your wrist to send the ball crosscourt (figure 10.4b).

a   *b*

Figure 10.4 Preparing for a straight drive *(a)*, and then hitting a crosscourt drive *(b)*.

Misstep
Your opponent easily reads your shots when you try to hit with deception.

Correction
You are probably trying to use deception too much, or you are setting up in such an exaggerated manner that it gives away to your opponent that you are trying to deceive him.

DISGUISE AND DECEPTION DRILLS

Besides the drills that follow, you can use many other drills in this book to practice deception and disguise. The drills involving more than one person provide an opportunity to hit with various racket preparations and body positions. Use the drills that offer you a choice of shots to see if you can wrong-foot your partner.

Disguise and Deception Drill 1. *Straight or Crosscourt?*

Your partner stands in the backcourt and hits a boast. Move forward from the T and hit either a straight or crosscourt drive. Try to use disguise or deception to wrong-foot your partner. Your partner should watch carefully and try to keep the drill going by returning your shot with another boast. Play for 3 minutes.

To Increase Difficulty

- Allow your partner to hit drops or boasts.
- Confine your crosscourt shot to a lob.

Success Check

- Hold your shots.
- Use various body positions.
- Use your wrist.

Score Your Success

Wrong-foot your partner more than five times in 3 minutes = 10 points

Wrong-foot your partner four or five times in 3 minutes = 5 points

Wrong-foot your partner fewer than four times in 3 minutes = 1 point

Your score ___

Disguise and Deception Drill 2. *Crosscourt or Drop?*

Your partner stands in a back corner and hits a boast. Stand in the front corner and hit either a straight drop or a crosscourt drive. Your partner should move up to the T after the boast and try to return your crosscourt with a boast or your drop with another drop. Your goal is to hit your shot with as much deception as possible, trying to wrong-foot your partner. Play this as a game. You score a point if your shot is unreturnable, and your partner scores a point by successfully returning your shot. Play to 11 points.

To Increase Difficulty

- Have your partner hit either a boast or a straight drop.

To Decrease Difficulty

- Have your partner hit a straight drop instead of a boast.

Success Check

- Use a short backswing.
- Hold your shot.
- Use your wrist on the crosscourt shot.

Score Your Success

Beat your partner = 5 points

Your score ___

Disguise and Deception Drill 3. *Deceive With the Boast*

With a partner, play a rally in the back corner, hitting straight drives and circling around each other as in Moving and Hitting in the Backcourt Drill 4, backcourt rallying, in step 4 (page 59). You also are allowed to use boasts, but use them sparingly. Hit with disguise and deception to try to send your opponent the wrong way. Play a game in which the drives must hit beyond the short line and no farther from the side wall than the width of the service box. If you play a boast that your partner is unable to return, you win the point. Your partner scores a point by returning the boast with any shot. Play to 11 points on the forehand side, and then play a second game to 11 points on the backhand side.

To Increase Difficulty

- Allow your partner to hit a boast shot, too.

Success Check

- Prepare your racket high.
- Wait as long as possible before striking the ball.
- Use the same body position for both boasts and drives.

Score Your Success

Beat your partner on the forehand side = 5 points

Beat your partner on the backhand side = 5 points

Your score ___

SUCCESS SUMMARY
FOR DISGUISE AND DECEPTION

After you have a firm grasp of the basics of good stroke production and movement, you're ready to elevate your play in other ways. To keep good players from anticipating your shots, you need to develop tactics of disguise and deception. Although these two aspects differ, you will use both to keep your opponent guessing throughout the match.

With disguise, make no definite racket or position moves until the last moment, but be sure you know where you want to hit the ball. With deception, you must be ready to use more wrist than normal to direct the ball in a way other than what your racket and body position indicate. These techniques require a great deal of experimentation and practice. You should use them sparingly.

Before moving on to step 11, Match Play, evaluate how you did on the drills in this step. Tally your scores to determine how well you have mastered disguise and deception. If you scored 15 points or more, you are ready to move on to step 11. If you did not score at least 15 points, practice the drills again until you raise your scores before moving on to step 11.

Disguise and Deception Drills

1. Straight or Crosscourt?	___ out of 10
2. Crosscourt or Drop?	___ out of 5
3. Deceive With the Boast	___ out of 10
Total	___ *out of 25*

It is now time to move on from shot making to learning match tactics. Step 11 introduces basic tactics you should use as you play a match. It will take you through how to prepare for a match to what you should be thinking about during the match. It is very important to enter every match with some type of game plan. This step will help you develop that game plan.

Match Play

Learning good technique and movement will certainly help you on your path toward excelling at squash. But when you watch a squash match, you'll often see a player with superior fitness and shot play lose. This occurs because the opponent was better prepared for the match and was more knowledgeable about strategic play.

Shot selection in squash is critical. Having good technique isn't worth much if you play the wrong shot in a particular situation and leave yourself helplessly out of position. Good strategy comes from being well prepared and having some basic principles to fall back on in times of need.

When you step on court to begin a match, think about trying to establish your basic game. This involves pinning your opponent into the back corners with solid drives. Once you establish your basic game, begin to hit more to the frontcourt to work your opponent around the court. Always remember the three basic good habits:

1. Watch the ball.
2. Move to the T.
3. Prepare your racket early.

Remember that if things aren't going your way, you should try something different to break your opponent's rhythm.

PREPARE FOR THE MATCH

Develop a prematch routine that will allow you to step on court in a relaxed, yet focused, manner. Arrive for your match with plenty of time to change, warm up, and check which court you're playing on. This last point is particularly important if you're playing at a club for the first time or if you're playing in a tournament in which you may not learn your court assignment until you arrive at the club. Allow at least 15 minutes to

warm up; see step 13 for examples of exercises to do during your warm-up. During this time, begin to focus on the match. Positive thinking at this stage, particularly if you're nervous about the upcoming match, can help you get into the right mind-set for the game.

Check out the court conditions because the temperature will affect the bounce of the ball. If the court is hot, you can expect a match with long, drawn-out rallies. You'll need to be prepared to concentrate for long periods to avoid making unforced errors. If the court is cold, the ball likely will be slower and the rallies, shorter. In this situation, you should be ready to play very tight squash. Any loose shots will be dispatched easily for winners. Make full use of the 5-minute on-court warm-up period to groove your strokes and check out your opponent.

ESTABLISH YOUR BASIC GAME

Once the match begins, your main priority should be to establish your basic game—hitting good, solid drives deep into the back corners. This should help settle your nerves and get you into the rhythm of the game. Make your opponent work for the first few points. Don't hit too many shots to the frontcourt where you risk making errors. Nothing is worse than falling behind in the first game by making a series of unforced errors. Also, early on in the match your opponent will be fresh and able to run down your shots to the front corners. If you can keep your opponent on his heels at the back of the court, your frontcourt shots later in the match will be more effective.

WORK YOUR OPPONENT AROUND THE COURT

Once you have established your basic game, begin to introduce more shots to the frontcourt to move your opponent up and down the court. In particular, look for opportunities to move your opponent from one back corner to the opposite front corner and vice versa. Do this, for example, by pushing your opponent forward with a drop and then driving the return to the opposite back corner. Or cut out one of your opponent's drives from the back with a drop volley or a boast.

Try to get away from the idea of hitting outright winners. Instead, look to create shot combinations that put your opponent so out of position that you can win the point by hitting to the open court.

BE READY TO PLAY DEFENSIVELY AND OFFENSIVELY IN EVERY RALLY

Of course, when you are faced with a challenging opponent, you will not always be able to dictate the rallies and work your opponent around the court. At times your opponent will be working you! Therefore, in every rally, you must be ready to play defensively when under pressure but be able to switch to a more offensive mode as soon as the opportunity arises.

Generally, you should play defensively if you are feeling rushed as you approach the ball or if your opponent has hit a shot to any of the four corners that is tight to the side wall. Even under pressure, try to stay poised and patient. Don't try to be too clever. Instead, focus on keeping your shots straight and tight to the side wall to limit your opponent's opportunities to volley the ball and thus increase the pressure on you. If you must hit crosscourt, make sure you hit your shot with good width so that it takes your opponent away from the T. Strive to get the ball past your opponent into the back corners because this will allow you to regain the T and relieve the pressure at least temporarily.

From the back corners, boast only if you cannot hit a straight shot, and try to keep your boasts low on the front wall to avoid setting up your opponent for an easy drop shot or kill shot to the front corners. If you are under pressure in the frontcourt, try to avoid the temptation to attempt to get out of trouble by hitting the ball as hard as you can, especially crosscourt. A good opponent will be waiting for this and will step up and volley the ball past you before you have time to react. Instead, your best options from the front are a clinging straight drop shot or, if you are too off balanced to execute that shot, a high crosscourt lob. It is critical that your lob be high enough that your opponent cannot volley it. Another good option is a slow, looping straight drive. This shot will need to stay tight to the side wall, especially if you sense that your opponent is well positioned close behind you.

As soon as the opening arises, switch from defense to offense and start pressuring your opponent. When on the attack, stay up in the court around the short line to pounce on your opponent's weak returns. Try to get in a comfort zone in which your body is loose and you feel in such control that all four corners seem inviting for your next shot. Apply pressure by taking the ball early and injecting pace or through deft touches to the front corners.

If you are struggling to find the openings to attack and feel constantly under pressure, try to move up behind your opponent and look for an opportunity to hit a quick volley or half volley. If you can whip a volley low and hard, either straight or crosscourt, it may surprise

your opponent and force her off balance for her next shot. If you do force a weak shot from your opponent, your instincts may be to go for a winner immediately, given the pressure you have been under. But the smart player resists this temptation and instead drives the ball deep to establish herself in the comfort zone.

If you are finding opportunities hard to come by, another way of switching from defense to offense is to wait for a slightly overhit drive from your opponent that sits a little higher off the back wall. Try to hit a medium-paced crosscourt shot high on the front wall and wide enough that it hits high on the side wall around the back of the service box. As long as your crosscourt has enough width, it will be difficult for your opponent to cut out on the volley. As your shot comes off the side wall, it will lose momentum as it approaches the back wall. This type of shot often forces the opponent into hitting either a boast to the frontcourt or a weak drive. Try to capitalize on this with your next shot by taking the ball early and hitting a soft drop shot tight into one of the front corners.

TAKE CALCULATED RISKS

To keep your opponent under pressure, you need to take some risks. The best players, though, take only calculated risks. During a rally, the opportunity to attack the ball will arise. Given the speed of the game, you must make a split-second decision: Do you go for a potential winner and risk hitting the tin, or hit a safer shot to the back of the court?

During the rally, think about these questions to determine how risky a shot you are willing to try:

- Are you well positioned on the T?
- Are you technically set up to be able to execute the risky shot?
- Do you have the momentum and confidence to execute the risky shot?
- Is your opponent out of position?
- Can you hit the shot with deception or disguise?
- If your opponent gets to your shot, will he likely have limited shot selection in response?

- Will you be able to respond to his next shot, or will you be left hopelessly out of position?
- Do you have enough space to execute the shot?
- Does the score allow you to try a risky shot in this rally?

If you are not well positioned on the T with your racket up early, you are more likely to hit a poorly executed shot and lose the advantage if you attempt a risky winner. Similarly, you are likely to miss if you are not confident about the shot you are about to attempt. In these situations, be more cautious and try to keep the pressure on your opponent with a shot to the back corners. It is very important to consider what your opponent will be able to do if your execution is not perfect and she can get to your shot. Is she so out of position that you likely will still have the advantage? Or if she gets to your shot, will she have an easy winner because you will be out of position? If it is the former, you should go for the winner, but if it is the latter, it is a poor risk to take so you should consider a more cautious shot.

The match situation is important as well. If you are up in the match, you might be more inclined to take risks because this will keep the pressure on your opponent. If you are a long way down in the match, it may make sense to take some risks to try to change the momentum. But in a tight match, especially near the end of each game, every rally is critical and you cannot afford to take too many risks.

CHANGE A LOSING GAME

The old adage "never change a winning game, but always change a losing one" definitely applies to squash. If you're winning, keep plugging away with the same strategy. You don't want to risk giving away the winning position by changing your strategy. On the other hand, if you're losing, try different tactics to break your opponent's rhythm.

One particularly good strategy is to change the pace of the game. Slow down the game by hitting more lobs, or, if the game is already at a slow pace, speed it up by volleying more and hitting harder drives. You could also change the game by trying to attack more. If you're losing because you're making too many mistakes, try to extend the rallies by hitting more shots to the back of the court.

One situation in which you may not want to change strategy when losing is when you're playing a clearly superior opponent. In this type of match, don't become disheartened. Instead, look at the match as a challenge and a way to improve your game. Try not to give your opponent easy points by constantly going for winners. Keep the rallies going as long as you can, making your opponent work hard for each point. You may find that by doing this you lose by a larger margin, but you should be able to keep your opponent on court longer. In the long run, this will be more beneficial to your game.

MAINTAIN YOUR COMPOSURE

Squash can test your mental patience to its limit. In the heat of battle, it is easy to let a few breaks that go against you, such as a referee's call or a lucky shot from your opponent, upset you and cause you to lose concentration. When you play, focus on your own game and try to ignore external factors as much as possible. Rarely will external factors determine the outcome of a match unless you allow them to. Concentrate all your effort on what you can control.

Showing anger toward the referee or your opponent is also extremely unsporting. Remember that normally the referee is working voluntarily and is doing the best job he can. Also, squash should be fun for you and your opponent. It is not much fun to play against someone who is constantly ranting and raving. Try to keep your emotions to yourself, stay composed, and concentrate on the match at hand.

FOSTER THE THREE
MOST IMPORTANT HABITS

Squash is a difficult game to master. Improvement often takes much time and practice. Gradually try to incorporate some of the ideas discussed in this book about stroke production and movement. Trying to do too much too quickly, however, may have a negative effect on your game. Begin by fostering three basic good habits:

1. **Watch the ball.** This is particularly important when your opponent is hitting out of the back corners. Don't stare at the front wall. Turn and watch your opponent strike the ball. This will give you the time you need to retrieve the shot.

2. **Move to the T.** After you've played your shot, don't just stand waiting until your

opponent hits the ball. Instead, move to the T so you can cover all four corners.

3. **Prepare the racket early.** As soon as you decide whether you're going to hit a forehand or a backhand, begin to prepare the racket. Getting the racket back early will help you move into the correct position to hit the ball and will give you more time to get to your opponent's shots.

Match Play Drill 1. *Pressure Drills*

Have a partner stand in the right back corner and hit boasts, drops, or straight drives. You must retrieve your partner's shots with drives back to your partner in the right back corner. Keep the drill going continuously as long as you can, using the lob to slow down the exercise if necessary. This exercise puts you under the sort of pressure you might face in your toughest matches. Repeat the drill with your partner switching to the left back corner.

To Increase Difficulty

- Your partner stands in the backcourt and hits boasts, drops, or drives. You can hit only straight drives.

To Decrease Difficulty

- Your partner hits only drops or drives, no boasts.
- Your partner alternates hitting boasts, drops, and drives, in that order.

Success Check

- Watch the ball.
- Recover to the T.
- Lob when you are under pressure.

Score Your Success

Keep the exercise going hitting shots to the right back corner for more than 5 minutes = 10 points

Keep the exercise going hitting shots to the right back corner for 3 to 5 minutes = 5 points

Keep the exercise going hitting shots to the right back corner for less than 3 minutes = 1 point

Keep the exercise going hitting shots to the left back corner for more than 5 minutes = 10 points

Keep the exercise going hitting shots to the left back corner for 3 to 5 minutes = 5 points

Keep the exercise going hitting shots to the left back corner for less than 3 minutes = 1 point

Your score ___

Match Play Drill 2. *Conditioned Backcourt Game*

Play a conditioned, or modified, game in which your opponent can play any shot, but you must hit all your shots to bounce past the short line. You may find yourself struggling to win rallies against a strong partner. Try to set realistic targets. If you aren't winning many points, concentrate on keeping the rallies going. Play one game to 11 points with point-per-rally scoring.

To Increase Difficulty

- Besides hitting all your shots past the short line, you must hit all your shots straight.

To Decrease Difficulty

- You must hit all shots past the short line except for one type of shot. For example, hit all shots past the short line except for the forehand boast, which can bounce in front of the short line.

Success Check

- Concentrate on good width.
- Keep changing the pace.
- Try to be patient.

Score at least 7 points against your opponent = 5 points

Score 5 or 6 points against your opponent = 3 points

Score fewer than 5 points against your opponent = 1 point

Your score ___

Match Play Drill 3. *Conditioned Volley Game*

Play a conditioned, or modified, game in which you must not let the ball hit the back wall. If it does, you immediately lose the point. During this game you must stay alert and prepare the racket early so you can cut off your opponent's shots in the midcourt area. Also, the deeper in the court you keep your opponent, the harder you make it for your opponent to drive the ball past you. Play one game to 11 points with point-per-rally scoring.

To Decrease Difficulty

- Have your opponent play with the same shot restriction.

Success Check

- Prepare your racket early.
- Volley at every opportunity.
- Keep your opponent deep.

Score Your Success

Score at least 7 points against your opponent = 5 points

Score 5 or 6 points against your opponent = 3 points

Score fewer than 5 points against your opponent = 1 point

Your score ___

Match Play Drill 4. *Short Handicap Games*

The object of these games is to put you into the pressure of end-of-game situations. Play a game to 5 points with point-per-rally scoring. The player who loses the game begins the next game a point ahead (at 1-0). If the same player loses the next game, that player starts the third game 2 points ahead. If the player who loses the first two games wins the third, that player would go back to being just 1 point ahead for the fourth game (fourth game begins at 1-0). Keep playing games in this fashion. If a player starts a game at 3-0 and loses, then the player who won the game starts the next game with –1 (negative 1). If you know at the start that you and your partner differ in ability, you may want to begin the first game with the weaker player leading by whatever you agree is an appropriate margin. Play as many games as you can in 30 minutes.

Success Check

- Keep unforced errors to a minimum.
- Play every rally as if you are game point down.
- Establish a strong basic game.

Score Your Success

Win more games than your opponent = 5 points

Your score ___

152

Match Play Drill 5. *Three-Quarter Court*

Play a rally in which one of the back quarters of the court is out of court. You can play this game with any number of players. The players not involved in the rally line up in the back corner, which isn't in play. The winner of the rally stays on and receives in the next rally. The loser of the rally joins the end of the line, and the player at the front of the line serves in the next rally. Keep score, 1 point for every rally you win. Play until one player reaches 11 points. Then switch sides so the opposite back corner is out of court.

To Increase Difficulty

- Instead of using three-quarters of the court, use only one-half of the court, either the forehand side or the backhand side.

Success Check

- Watch the ball.
- Move to the T.
- Prepare your racket early.

Score Your Success

Be the first to score 11 points with the left back corner out of play = 5 points

Be the first to score 11 points with the right back corner out of play = 5 points

Your score ___

SUCCESS SUMMARY FOR MATCH PLAY

The culmination of all your basic learning comes with match and tournament play. Yet the player who doesn't prepare properly for a match or doesn't choose shots wisely during the match can waste strong fundamentals. Always remember the habits to foster on the squash court—watch the ball, prepare your racket early, and move back to the T after each shot.

The only way to get comfortable playing under match conditions is to go out and play. When playing tournaments, keep in mind that you and your opponent should be having fun. Maintaining a good sporting attitude on the court will help ensure this.

Before moving on to step 12, Advanced Tactics, evaluate how you did on the drills in this step. Tally your scores to determine how well you have mastered match play. If you scored 30 points or more, you are ready to move on to step 12. If you did not score at least 30 points, practice the drills again until you raise your scores before moving on to step 12.

Match Play Drills

1. Pressure Drills	___ out of 20	
2. Conditioned Backcourt Game	___ out of 5	
3. Conditioned Volley Game	___ out of 5	
4. Short Handicap Games	___ out of 5	
5. Three-Quarter Court	___ out of 10	
Total	___ *out of 45*	

Step 12 introduces more advanced match tactics. Specifically, you will learn to evaluate the type of opponent you are up against and develop strategies that you can use against each type of player. As important as it is to establish your own basic game in a match, it is equally important to be able to adapt that basic game during a match to blunt the tactics that your opponent is using against you. Step 12 will help you do this.

Advanced Tactics

On a squash court, you will encounter a wide variety of player types, from the hard hitter to the soft lob and drop expert. Some players keep the rallies long and seem to be able to run all day without tiring, whereas others go for winners almost from the start of every rally. It is important to quickly identify the style of your opponent, evaluate his strengths and weaknesses, and adapt your game accordingly.

Look for clues as to how your opponent plays from the moment you step on court. In the warm-up, watch the rotation of the hips, trunk, and shoulders as your opponent sets up and strikes the ball. Look at the shots she plays from various positions. Ask yourself, does she have a short backswing? Does she strike the ball flat or with slice? Does she snap at the ball behind her? How does she cope with hard-hit shots or with lobs high on the side wall? Does she change her grip in certain positions on the court? How

does she approach the ball in the front and back corners? Does she have a tendency to get too close to the ball? Are her feet too close together to have good technique? Does she tend to hit with an open or closed stance? Does she hit hard from the backcourt, or does she tend to chip or float shots to the back?

The more analysis you do in the warm-up, the better prepared you will be to adapt your game from the very first point. Every player is unique, so it is down to you to process this information and be aware of tactical changes you need to make to adjust to your opponent. When played at a fairly equal level, squash is a very challenging game. Subtleties in the flow of the game make it unique. Players must calculate all the time how they can get one step ahead of their opponents in this battle of wits. This step presents ideas of what to do and what to avoid when faced with various types of opponents.

HARD HITTER

The hard hitter will try to overpower you. He constantly hits the ball as hard as he can and plays with high intensity. He will put you on the defensive, send you off balance, and make you rush your shots.

However, the hard hitter often lacks control. Most shots are hit low on the front wall and many end up in the midcourt area. It is critical not to panic and patiently work the hard hitter around the court. Trying to hit the ball hard all the time is very tiring. As long as you are not overpowered and can keep rallies going, normally you can outlast this opponent.

Try This

- Stay up in the court and do not allow the hard hitter to dominate the T. It will be a difficult match if you are forced to play consistently out of the back corners. Volley as many shots as possible to keep this opponent away from the middle of the court.

- Vary the pace of your shots. Don't get dragged into trying to overpower the hard hitter. Use slow chip shots, especially crosscourt, to take your opponent away from the T.

- Use a lob serve more than you might usually. The hard hitter likes a fast tempo, so setting a slower tone early in the rally can unsettle him. Normally, the hard hitter does not have great control when forced to hit high volleys because he is trying to hit the shot too hard.

- Keep the ball deep and tight to force the hard hitter to boast. Because this opponent uses a big swing to generate pace, he normally has great difficulty retrieving the ball out of the back corners except with a hard-hit and normally loose boast that will give you opportunities at the front of the court to hit easy winners.

- Think hard about smart placement of your shots. Normally, you don't need to go for many outright winners to beat this opponent. If you can move him around the court, he will get tired, start making errors, and eventually start beating himself.

Avoid This

- Do not hit drop shots unless you force the hard hitter to hit a weak boast. If you have not forced a weak shot out of the back court, it is likely the ball will come too quickly to enable you to execute a tight drop shot. Also, a hard hitter normally is much better when moving up into the front court where he can use his big swing rather than backpedaling to retrieve shots hit deep in the corners.

- Do not be lured into taking unnecessary risks. The longer the match is, the more likely the hard hitter is to slow down and start making errors. If you try to end rallies too soon by going for high-risk shots, you will make the errors and put the hard hitter in the driver's seat.

- Do not show signs of frustration. The hard hitter is trying to overwhelm you. Any indications that he is achieving this will make him stronger and harder to break down. Be patient.

Advanced Tactics Drill 1. *North Versus South*

Play a conditioned, or modified, game in which you must hit everything above the service line (north) and your partner must hit everything below the service line (south). In addition, your partner must hit only hard shots—no drops or soft boasts—although hard-hit boasts are allowed. You always serve regardless of who won the last rally. Play three games using point-per-rally scoring to 11 points.

To Increase Difficulty

- Allow your partner to hit a set number of soft shots per rally. Start at one soft shot per rally and increase the number of soft shots to further increase the level of difficulty.

To Decrease Difficulty

- Restrict your partner to hitting only a set number of boasts per rally. Start at a maximum of three boasts per rally and reduce that number to zero to further decrease the level of difficulty.

Success Check

- Use a lob serve.
- Keep the ball deep and tight to try to force you partner to boast.
- Try to be patient.

Win two or three games against your partner = 5 points

Win one game against your partner = 3 points

Your score ____

DROP-LOBBER

The drop-lobber will try to wear you out by running you to all four corners of the court. She is an expert in ball control and working the point. The drop-lobber's game plan is to wait for you to get tired and frustrated. She is able to exploit players who have weak frontcourt games. Often, the drop-lobber is an older player who has acquired great racket skills and a very strong understanding of the tactics of the game over the years. She often will appear perfectly positioned for every shot you hit. But she is likely not fast around the court and probably lacks fitness. If you can get her moving, she will become a much easier opponent to play against.

Try This

- Keep up on the short line as much as possible, constantly watching for your opponent to hit a drop shot (you will likely not have to wait long!). If you can get on to your opponent's drop shot fast, you should be able to control the rallies. The problem arises if you stand too far back or are slow off the mark and end up off balance and at full stretch trying to return your opponent's drop shots.

- If you can, redrop your opponent's drop shot. The drop-lobber will be looking for a hard-hit return and likely will not be fast enough to get up to your drop.

- Watch this opponent's racket face very carefully. She often will give you a clue that a drop is coming by dropping the racket face or by opening the face to get more slice.

- Make sure your serves hit the side wall. The drop-lobber will look to volley her return of serve as much as possible to take the initiative in the rally. It is much harder to volley drop a return of serve when the ball is coming off the side wall, so it will be easier for you to avoid ceding control early in the rally. This alone often quickly blunts the drop-lobber's game plan.

- From the backcourt, use more tight chip drives that loop the ball into the back corners. These shots give this opponent less power to play off of and so make hitting a drop shot winner a lot harder.

- From the midcourt area, use more pace on your shots. This will keep your opponent off balance, making drop shots more difficult to execute.

Avoid This

- Do not hit a drop shot if you are off balance. Hitting a drop shot from an off-balanced position will likely set up your opponent to lob you to the back and put you under even more pressure. If you are too stretched in the frontcourt to hit a tight drop shot, hit a high lob.

- Do not try to be fancy when you get to your opponent's drop shot. It's easy to make a mistake if you try to be too cute when a simple tight drop shot return is all you need to take control of the rally.

- Do not show your frustration. This is an experienced player who will thrive on seeing you angry with yourself!

Advanced Tactics Drill 2. *Drop-Lob Conditioned Game*

Play a conditioned, or modified, game in which your partner can hit only drop or lob shots. You can play normally, except you must follow any drop shot from your partner with your own straight drop shot. Play three games using point-per-rally scoring to 11 points.

To Increase Difficulty

- Allow your partner to hit a set number of boasts per rally in addition to drops and lobs. Start at one boast per rally and increase the number of boasts to further increase the level of difficulty.

To Decrease Difficulty

- Remove the restriction that you must hit a drop shot after your partner hits a drop shot.

Success Check

- Keep up on the short line as much as you can.
- Volley your partner's lobs whenever possible.
- Keep up the pace.

Score Your Success

Win two or three games against your partner = 5 points

Win one game against your partner = 3 points

Your score ___

RUNNER

The runner is fast around the court and has great endurance. Usually he is not very good at hitting winners but instead wins matches by keeping the rallies going and wearing down his opponents. The runner relies on forcing opponents to make mistakes, often by luring them into trying risky shots because they are frustrated at their inability to end the rally. The runner is accustomed to playing long matches.

Try This

- Be patient and work the point. Do not try for a winner until you have hit at least four shots to the backcourt.
- Look for opportunities to volley. This will open up the rallies a bit more and lead to more openings to hit winners.
- Use drop shots and boasts to work this opponent forward. The runner is less likely to hit a winner, so you can afford to hit shots to the front a little higher above the tin to avoid making mistakes. However, try to keep shots tight to the side wall so that you use the shots to the front to work an opening.
- Hit tight, straight drives rather than crosscourt drives. This will reduce the angles that your opponent can use against you and will prevent him from using his speed as effectively.

- Try to use more touch or angle on your volleys to keep the runner off balance.
- Hold your shots more and try to use deception. The runner likes a more straightforward rally and can be wrong-footed easily. He is less likely to punish you with a winner if your attempt at deception leads to a slightly looser shot than you would ideally like to hit.

Avoid This

- Do not get lured into going for winners immediately to avoid long rallies. It cannot be stressed enough that you need to be patient against this type of player. He is relying on you to make mistakes. If you go for a winner before creating a good opening, mistakes will inevitably follow.
- Do not get discouraged if he runs down shots that are winners against most of your other opponents. Keep working at it. If you can control rallies and keep him moving, even the runner will eventually get tired and start to make errors.
- Do not go for shots that you do not feel comfortable executing no matter how frustrated you feel about your inability to end the rally. Play within yourself.

Advanced Tactics Drill 3. *Two-on-One, Straight Drives and Boasts Only*

Play a conditioned, or modified, game against a team of two other players. You play normally, but the team of two players can hit only straight drives or boasts. One of the team members covers the forehand side of the court; the other covers the backhand side. When they are serving, the nonserver on the team stands behind the server. When you are serving, the nonreceiver on the team stands behind you. Serving works the same as in a regular game—serve until you lose a rally, and then the other team serves until it loses a rally. For the team, one player serves continually until the team loses a rally. The next time they are up to serve, the other player serves, again continually until the team loses a rally. Play three games using point-per-rally scoring to 11 points.

To Increase Difficulty

- Allow the team to hit straight drops as well.

To Decrease Difficulty

- Restrict the team to hitting only a set number of boasts per rally. Start at a maximum of three boasts per rally and reduce that number to zero to further decrease the level of difficulty.

Success Check

- Hit straight drives rather than crosscourt drives.
- Use the drop and boast to work the team up and down the court.
- Be patient and work the rallies.

Score Your Success

Win two or three games against the team = 5 points

Win one game against the team = 3 points

Your score ___

COUNTER-PUNCHER

In some regards the counter-puncher is similar to the runner. Normally, she is fit and fast around the court. She doesn't have the racket skills to hit outright winners easily, but instead likes to play mainly around the midcourt with her opponent in front and take advantage of any loose shots her opponent hits. A favorite tactic is to draw her opponent to the front with a drop or boast and then look to aggressively pounce on the weak return. Normally, the counter-puncher thrives against an attacker (see next section) because, when going for a winner, the attacker often puts herself out of position for the return shot, if the counter-puncher gets the shot back. The counter-puncher is quick and will get to a lot more shots than most opponents so she quickly can turn a defensive position into an offensive one. Many tactics that work well against the runner will also work against the counter-puncher.

Try This

- Be selective when you are moved to the front of the court. Mainly hit drops and

lobs. The counter-puncher is waiting for a hard-hit drive, especially crosscourt, so never hit that shot!

- Use drop shots and boasts to move the counter-puncher to the frontcourt. This player typically is not very comfortable hitting from the frontcourt unless she has her opponent out of position.

- When you have her at the front, stay up in the court fairly close behind to pressure her. Force her to beat you with a lob from the front as opposed to giving her opportunities to drive the ball past you.

- Keep the ball tight along the side walls. The counter-puncher is looking to use the angles created by crosscourt shots to hit passing shots by you.

- Try to hold your shots and use deception, and use more angle and touch on your volleys to keep the counter-puncher off balance. If you become too predictable, she will run down your shots and beat you with quick, hard-hit, low drives that will be past you before you have time to react.

Avoid This

- Do not supply the counter-puncher with a lot of pace to work with. She prefers the ball coming with speed because this creates the best opportunities to counter-punch.

- Do not hit hard serves only. It is especially important to mix up the pace of your serves. If you constantly hit hard serves, your opponent will have the opportunity to counter-punch right from the beginning of the rally.

- Do not attempt winners unless you feel confident that you can recover to the T before the counter-puncher hits her return. This way, if she does hit your shot back, you will still be in position to stay in the rally as opposed to allowing her an easy put-away.

Advanced Tactics Drill 4.   *Two-on-One, No Back Wall and Below Service Line*

Play a conditioned, or modified, game against a team of two other players, similar to the last drill. Again, you play normally, but this time the team of two must hit every shot, except the serve, below the service line. Also, the team of two loses the point if any of your shots hit the back wall. These rules encourage the team to hit boasts and drops to move you to the front and then to cut off your returns with hard, low drives. The team also must take the ball early to keep it from hitting the back wall. Play three games using point-per-rally scoring to 11 points.

To Increase Difficulty

- Take away the restriction that the team loses the rally if your shot hits the back wall.

To Decrease Difficulty

- Restrict the team to hitting only a set number of boasts per rally. Start at a maximum of three boasts per rally and reduce that number to zero to further decrease the level of difficulty.

Success Check

- Avoid hitting hard crosscourt shots.
- Keep your shots tight to the side walls.
- Slow down the pace.

Score Your Success

Win two or three games against the team = 5 points

Win one game against the team = 3 points

Your score ___

ATTACKER

The attacker goes for lots of winners using a frontal attack and relies exclusively on his weapons as opposed to exploiting your weaknesses. This opponent often hits the ball hard and volleys a lot. After serving, he will step up and look to volley your return. When returning serve, he stands up in the court and hits lots of kill shots, a special favorite being the crosscourt volley kill shot into the nick. The key to beating this opponent is to hit very tight serves and returns of serve. Normally, if you can get into a rally, you will win the point because this opponent will get frustrated and make errors. It is important to understand that he is going to hit a lot of winners during the match and will likely be very streaky. But he also will be prone to hitting shots in the tin and is likely to run out of steam if you extend the rallies.

Try This

- Make sure your serves hit the side wall before your opponent can volley the ball. This will make it much harder for the attacker to hit a winner with his return of serve and thus get you into a rally. Once a rally has developed, your chances of winning the point increase.

- After your serve, stay up in the court and look for the kill shot from your opponent. You can do nothing about it if he hits a kill shot that rolls out of the nick. But if your serve is tight, his kill shot often will sit up a little. If you can get on to it quickly and hit a straight drop, it may lead to an easy winner because this opponent rarely follows up to the front of the court quickly.
- Hit your returns of serve straight and low. The attacker will seize on crosscourt shots, hitting a straight kill shot that will force you to run the diagonal of the court to stay in the rally.
- Try to step up and hit returns of serve early. Use a shorter backswing and a fast, punchy stroke to hit a hard, low return. This will reduce the time your opponent has to set up and will make it harder for him to hit a good volley on his next shot.
- Lob some returns. The attacker tends to move forward after serving. A good lob return will force him to backpedal. Also, most attackers hit great volleys off hard-hit crosscourt shots or loose straight drives but do not volley as well when moving backward and when the ball is high above their heads. Often, they will attempt low-percentage winners from very difficult positions, leading them to hit the tin.

Avoid This

- Do not get lured into staying back in the court and trying to hit hard returns past your opponent. Usually, the attacker is great at cutting off these shots on the volley and hitting a winner to the front corner.
- During the rally, do not let this opponent dominate the T. It is critically important to get in front of the attacker. If you allow him to dominate the front of the court, he will quickly finish you off by dispatching a string of kill shots into the front corners. Force him to hit winners from behind you. This will increase the chances of his hitting the tin or leaving a shot that sits up just enough for you to hit a drop shot.
- Do not get drawn into simply hacking at the ball as hard as you can. Although hitting with pace is important to give the attacker less time to set up for a possible winner, it is more important to hit tight. The attacker will be able to use your pace against you if your shots are loose, but if you can keep your shots tight, you will force your opponent to commit more errors.

Advanced Tactics Drill 5. *Two-on-One, Five-Shot Limit Per Rally*

Play a conditioned, or modified, game against a team of two other players, similar to the last two drills. Again, you play normally, but this time the team of two must hit every shot below the service line and so that the ball does not bounce beyond the short line. In addition, if you are able to extend the rally beyond five shots, you win the point. You always serve regardless of who won the last rally. These rules encourage the team to attack and try to end the rally as quickly as possible. Play three games using point-per-rally scoring to 11 points.

To Increase Difficulty

- Increase the shot limit per rally.

To Decrease Difficulty

- Do not allow the team to hit boasts.

Success Check

- Stay well up the court.
- Make sure your serves hit the side wall.
- Avoid hard-hit crosscourt shots.

Score Your Success

Win two or three games against the team = 5 points

Win one game against the team = 3 points

Your score ____

COMPLETE PLAYER

The complete player is the hardest to play against. This player is fit and fast. Her length is solid, and she attacks well when given the opening. She plays good shots from anywhere in the court and consequently provides the greatest tactical challenge. Keep in mind, though, that even a player who seems complete most certainly will execute some shots better than others. Every player struggles in some positions on the court. It is just a matter of maneuvering this opponent into these positions.

Try This

- Focus on playing to your strengths as much as possible.

- Even though your opponent may seem comfortable with all shots, watch carefully and try to discover any areas of weakness you can exploit. Varying your style during the match can help to identify your opponent's weaknesses.

- If you identify a weak point, keep hitting the ball to that area to exploit it as much as possible.

- Make sure you keep most of your shots deep and tight. This opponent will have the skills to take advantage of anything that you hit loose.

- Vary the pace of your basic drives. This opponent likely will play best if she has the chance to groove her shots off constant hard-hit drives.

- Challenge and attack this opponent with confidence at every opportunity. Even a seemingly complete player may become tentative suddenly if she perceives that her opponent is growing in confidence during the match.

Avoid This

- Do not idly sit by and let this opponent use her strengths throughout the match, even if those strengths play into the stronger parts of your game.

- Do not be lured into going for quick winners. Be patient, wait for opportunities to present themselves, and take only calculated risks.

- Do not show any signs of frustration. You will need all your mental strength to overcome such a talented and experienced opponent. This sort of player will feed off your frustration and grow even stronger and harder to break down.

Advanced Tactics Drill 6.   Two-on-One, No Restrictions

Play a game against a team of two other players, similar to the last three drills. This time there are no restrictions on either you or the team. This is the best way to simulate a game against the complete player. It may seem like a daunting task to win against two players. It certainly isn't easy, but it is not impossible. Try to follow some of the advice provided in this section, and see how many points you can win. Play three games using point-per-rally scoring to 11 points.

To Decrease Difficulty

- Give yourself an appropriate head start to make the games close. For example, you may begin at 5-0.

Success Check

- Play to your strengths.
- Vary the pace and style of your game.
- Attack with confidence.

Score Your Success

Win two or three games against the team = 10 points

Win one game against the team = 5 points

Your score ___

SUCCESS SUMMARY
FOR ADVANCED TACTICS

Focusing on a solid basic game will get you a long way in squash. However, it is important to understand how to make the necessary adaptations to deal with the styles of various opponents. Watch your opponent from the time you step on the court to gain clues as to how he might play. Constantly attempt to adapt your game to deal with the situation at hand. Remember, a player may change his style during a game, so be careful about getting locked into a strategy that is working well in the early part of the match but might not ultimately carry you through to victory.

Before moving on to step 13, Conditioning for Squash, evaluate how you did on the drills in this step. Tally your scores to determine how well you have mastered advanced tactics. If you scored 20 points or more, you are ready to move on to step 13. If you did not score at least 20 points, practice the drills again until you raise your scores before moving on to step 13.

Advanced Tactics Drills

1. North Versus South	___ out of 5	
2. Drop-Lob Conditioned Game	___ out of 5	
3. Two-on-One, Straight Drives and Boasts Only	___ out of 5	
4. Two-on-One, No Back Wall and Below Service Line	___ out of 5	
5. Two-on-One, Five-Shot Limit Per Rally	___ out of 5	
6. Two-on-One, No Restrictions	___ out of 10	
Total	___ **out of 35**	

Although playing squash is a great way to get fit, any serious squash player should work on conditioning off court to help improve her game. Step 13 highlights flexibility, speed, stamina, and strength—the key components of conditioning for squash. In the step you will also learn about building an off-season conditioning program.

Conditioning for Squash

There is an old adage, "Don't play squash to get fit. Instead, get fit to play squash." This is not entirely true because playing squash is an excellent way of getting and staying in shape. However, it is a fact that anyone who wants to be a serious squash player and play at a high level will need to dedicate some time outside of playing matches to work on conditioning.

Although it is possible to work on conditioning throughout the year, tournament players may not have time between tournaments during the main playing season to really focus on fit-

ness. Instead, many players opt to spend the season playing matches, practicing, and resting and save the hard conditioning work for the off-season.

The key components of conditioning necessary to improve play are flexibility, speed, stamina, and strength. It is important to work hard on each component if you are to become a complete player. This step highlights exercises that work on each component and lays out some training schedules for a solid off-season regiment to improve conditioning.

FLEXIBILITY

Stretching exercises improve flexibility and should be part of your warm-up routine before any match, practice session, or conditioning workout. Improving flexibility not only helps your movement around the court and your ability to bend down lower when striking the ball, but it also significantly decreases your risk of injury. It is important to go through a 15- to 20-minute stretching routine both before and after you play a match or do a conditioning workout.

Start your routine with some light aerobic exercises to get your muscles warm before you begin stretching. Taking a short jog, jumping

rope, riding a stationary bike, or executing some gently paced ghosting or court sprints are good examples of exercises that will get your muscles warm without risk of injury.

Static Stretches

After warming your muscles, begin with some static stretching. Static stretches require no movement, and the muscle stretch should be slow and gradual. Hold each stretch to a count of 10 and then relax. Perform each stretch two or three times in your session.

1. **Triceps stretch.** Pull the back of one elbow behind your head with your opposite arm (figure 13.1). Repeat on the other arm.

Figure 13.1   Triceps stretch.

2. **Shoulder stretch.** Lean into the side wall with your arm behind you at about a 90-degree angle (figure 13.2). Repeat on the other arm.

Figure 13.2   Shoulder stretch.

3. **Hamstring stretch.** Lie on your back. Pull your left knee to your chest and hold it with both hands. Stretch the right leg to full extension (figure 13.3). Repeat on the other leg.

Figure 13.3   Hamstring stretch.

4. **Quadriceps stretch.** Stand on one leg. Use a wall to support you, if necessary, and pull your foot up behind you with your hand (figure 13.4). Repeat on the other leg.

Figure 13.4   Quadriceps stretch.

5. Hip flexors and gluteus stretch. Step forward into a lunge position (figure 13.5). Hold; then repeat on the opposite leg.

Figure 13.5 Hip flexors and gluteus stretch.

6. Groin and inner thigh stretch. In a seated position, put the soles of your feet together. Hold your feet and push down with your knees (figure 13.6). Try not to bounce; instead, stretch slowly.

Figure 13.6 Groin and inner thigh stretch.

Dynamic Stretching

Follow static stretches with dynamic stretches. Dynamic stretches involve controlled, rhythmic movements. The movements are similar to those that you will make on a squash court. Perform each dynamic stretch for about 30 seconds, and repeat two or three times.

1. Bent-over trunk rotation. With your feet double shoulder-width apart, bend at the hips, ensuring that your spine stays long and your back doesn't round. Keep your knees slightly bent. Extend both arms out to your side at shoulder height. Rotate your trunk and arms and reach down toward your opposite foot with your hand while bending that leg and gently lunging to the side (figure 13.7). Alternate sides, keeping your arms straight at all times.

Figure 13.7 Bent-over trunk rotation.

2. High step with trunk rotation and opposite neck rotation. High step with your right knee while twisting your trunk to the right, reaching around your body with your arms and looking to the left. Repeat with a high step with your left knee while twisting your trunk to the left and reaching around your body with your arms and looking to the right (figure 13.8).

Figure 13.8 High step with trunk rotation and opposite neck rotation.

3. 45-degree crossover lunge with forehand and backhand swings. Stand with your feet shoulder-width apart similar to the ready position on the T. Take a long step forward with your left foot, crossing over your right foot to the 2 o'clock position. Gently swing your hand as if you were playing a forehand shot, if you are right-handed, or a backhand shot, if you are left-handed. Step back to the ready position, and then step forward with your right foot, crossing over your left foot to the 10 o'clock position. Pretend to play a backhand shot, if you are right-handed (figure 13.9), or a forehand shot, if you are left-handed.

Many static and dynamic stretches can be incorporated into your routine. The key is to make sure that you address each muscle group.

Figure 13.9 45-degree crossover lunge with backhand swing.

SPEED

The speed with which you can cover the court can have a huge impact on the amount of pressure you can exert on your opponent. If you move fast and can reach your opponent's shots quickly, you will have more options for your shots, and your opponent will be forced to take more risks than is prudent. It also allows you the possibility of recovering in a rally when you find yourself out of position.

Ghosting is a great way to improve speed, because it mirrors the movements you make during a match. Most players use ghosting as a core exercise during their training. Shuttle runs and interval sprints are also excellent ways to improve speed. If you are working with a partner, you can perform the shuttle runs as a race, and you can play other games such as squash ball recovery to work on your speed.

Ghosting

Ghosting exercises involve moving from the T to a corner or side, playing an imaginary stroke, and then moving back to the T. You can work on particular parts of the court (such as just the front or back corners), work on all parts of the court in one exercise, or randomly move to various areas of the court. The drills in

step 3 include more detail on specific ghosting exercises.

Shuttle Runs

Start a shuttle run by standing by the back wall. Run to the back of the service box, reach down to touch the floor, and then turn and run back to the back wall. Repeat by running to the short line, touching the floor, and then returning to the back wall. Finally, run and touch the front wall, and then return to the back wall. This completes one shuttle run (figure 13.10). Start by doing a set of five shuttle runs as quickly as you can. In future sessions, add additional sets with a minute rest between sets. You can also increase the number of shuttle runs in each set. Focus on speed. It is better to do more sets of fewer shuttle runs as quickly as you can, than to do too many shuttle runs in one set.

Interval Sprints

If you have access to one, a track is the best place to do interval sprints. If you do not have access to a track, use a large open space such as a park. Set cones around the track at roughly 50-meter intervals. Begin by gently jogging the first 50 meters. Once you reach the first cone, sprint

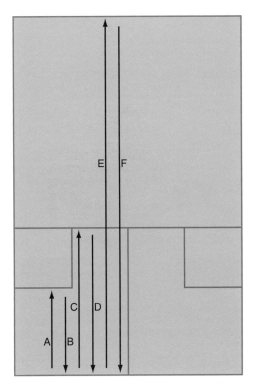

Figure 13.10 Shuttle run.

the 50 meters to the next cone. Jog the next 50 meters, giving yourself a chance to catch your breath. Sprint the next 50 meters, and so on. Start by doing a set that includes five sprints and five jogs. With each training session, try to increase the number of sprints until you reach 10. You can also make it harder by increasing the distance between the cones. Again, speed is the focus, so it is not advisable to increase the length of your sprints to anything greater than 100 meters each.

Squash Ball Recovery

Have a partner stand on the T with two or three balls. He throws one ball out toward a corner, and you run and try to pick up the ball before it hits the wall. Bring it back to your partner on the T. As you are bringing the ball back, your partner throws a ball to a different corner for you to chase down. The goal is for your partner to throw the ball with just enough speed to make you have to work as hard as possible to get each ball before it touches a wall. Continue the game for 2 minutes, and then switch roles.

STAMINA

Against an evenly matched opponent, endurance can be the critical factor that determines who wins and who loses. Thus, working on your stamina is crucial to enable you to pull out those long, hard-fought matches. All the exercises in the section on speed will improve stamina as well, especially as you increase the number of sets you complete in a single workout session.

Running longer distances is also a great way to improve stamina. The ideal distance to run is around 3 to 5 miles (4.8 to 8 km). If you cannot

manage that at first, begin by running 1 mile (1.6 km) and gradually increase the distance. In general, it is not helpful to run more than 5 miles (8 km) on a regular basis. Although it may help to improve your stamina, you run the risk of negatively affecting your speed around the court.

Jumping rope is another great exercise for building stamina. Start by jumping rope for 5 minutes. Gradually increase the amount of time until you can go for 10 to 15 minutes at a time.

STRENGTH

The final component of conditioning is strength. In particular, squash players should work on their upper-body and core strength. Lower-body strength tends to improve naturally from the exercises done to increase speed and stamina.

If you do not work to improve your core strength, you likely will find that during a long match your arms and shoulders begin to get tired and you have difficulty keeping good form with

your strokes. Although you can generate a significant amount of power from good stroke technique, you will find that improved core strength will lead to being able to hit the ball harder.

Various exercises can improve core strength. A number of machines often seen in weight rooms are specifically designed to improve upper-body strength. It is advisable at first to work with a personal trainer until you are comfortable that you are using the machines safely and for maximum benefit.

It is possible to build an adequate routine of strength exercises with only a pair of weights. For each of the following exercises, try to do three sets of 10 to 20 repetitions with a 20- to 30-second break between sets.

1. Push-ups. Start with your hands about shoulder-width apart and your palms on the floor, fingers stretched forward. Keeping your body straight, lower yourself until your face is close to the floor (figure 13.11). Pause at the bottom; then push up again.

Figure 13.11 Push-ups.

2. One-arm row. Support your body by placing your left hand and knee on a bench and have your right foot securely on the floor. Hold a weight in your right hand. With your back parallel to the floor, lift the weight by bending your arm and raising your elbow (figure 13.12). Pause when the weight reaches the side of your chest, and then slowly lower.

Figure 13.12 One-arm row.

3. Biceps curl. Start with your arms straight, palms turned up. Curl the weights up toward your shoulders (figure 13.13). Pause; then slowly lower them back to the starting position.

Figure 13.13 Biceps curl.

4. Triceps dip. Start with your hands behind you on a bench, on either side of your body, fingers facing forward. Bend your elbows and slowly lower your body (figure 13.14). Pause at the bottom of the movement; then push back up. Stop before your elbows reach a locked position, and repeat.

Figure 13.14 Triceps dip.

5. Breaststroke. Stand with your feet shoulder-width apart and your arms straight out in front of you. Hold a weight in each hand. Make smooth, circular breaststroke swimming movements, keeping your arms parallel to the floor at all times (figure 13.15).

Figure 13.15 Breaststroke.

6. Reverse flys. Lean forward on a slightly inclined bench. With your arms slightly bent, hold the weights close to the floor. Smoothly lift the weights until they are at shoulder height (figure 13.16). Pause; then slowly lower the weights to the starting position.

Figure 13.16 Reverse flys.

7. Lateral raises. Sit upright on a bench. Hold the weights at your sides. Keep your arms slightly bent, and slowly lift the weights to about shoulder height (figure 13.17). Pause; then slowly lower the weights to the starting position.

Figure 13.17 Lateral raises.

8. Bench flys. Lie on your back on a bench. Hold the weights above you. Slowly lower them to your sides, keeping your arms slightly bent at all times (figure 13.18). Stop when the weights are level with your shoulders. Pause; then return to the starting position.

Figure 13.18 Bench flys.

9. Shoulder press. Sit upright on an inclined bench to support your back. Start with your elbows bent, palms facing forward, and the weights just to the sides of your shoulders. Lift the weights from your shoulders above your head, keeping your palms facing forward at all times (figure 13.19). Pause when your elbows are almost straight; then lower the weights back down to the sides of your shoulders.

Figure 13.19 Shoulder press.

OFF-SEASON CONDITIONING PROGRAM FOR THE RECREATIONAL OR CLUB-LEVEL PLAYER

All players, from the novice to the serious club player, will find it worthwhile to take some time during the off-season to focus on conditioning. This is particularly important for players who play so much during the season that they have only limited time for workouts. Plan a schedule during the off-season that will address your conditioning goals. Space your workouts during the week so that you get plenty of rest between workouts. Even though your focus during this period may be on improving speed, strength, and stamina, try to play or practice at least once a week.

Always make sure you finish your conditioning program in time to allow yourself a few weeks to get back on court to work on your match play before the season really gets going again. Conditioning programs should last six to eight weeks and should be relatively easy to start, becoming more intense over time. Table 13.1 is an example of a six-week conditioning program for a club-level player. Each session is intended to last between an hour and an hour and a half, including the warm-up stretching at the beginning and the cool-down at the end.

Table 13.1 Off-Season Conditioning Program for the Recreational or Club-Level Player

	Monday	Tuesday	Wednesday	Thursday	Friday	Saturday	Sunday
Week 1	Stretch 15 min Run 2 mi (3.2 km) Strength 25 min Stretch 15 min	Rest	Stretch 15 min Run 1 mi (1.6 km) Jump rope 5 min Interval sprints 15 min Stretch 15 min	Squash game or practice	Rest	Stretch 15 min Ghosting 15 min Strength 25 min Stretch 15 min	Squash game or practice or rest
Week 2	Stretch 15 min Run 3 mi (4.8 km) Strength 25 min Stretch 15 min	Rest	Stretch 15 min Run 1 mi (1.6 km) Jump rope 5 min Shuttle run 10 min Stretch 15 min	Squash game or practice	Rest	Stretch 15 min Ghosting 15 min Strength 25 min Stretch 15 min	Squash game or practice or rest
Week 3	Stretch 15 min Run 4 mi (6.4 km) Strength 25 min Stretch 15 min	Rest	Stretch 15 min Run 2 mi (3.2 km) Jump rope 5 min Interval sprint 20 min Stretch 15 min	Squash game or practice	Rest	Stretch 15 min Ghosting 20 min Strength 25 min Stretch 15 min	Squash game or practice or rest
Week 4	Stretch 15 min Run 5 mi (8 km) Strength 25 min Stretch 15 min	Squash game or practice	Stretch 15 min Run 2 mi (3.2 km) Jump rope 5 min Shuttle run 15 min Stretch 15 min	Squash game or practice	Rest	Stretch 15 min Ghosting 20 min Strength 25 min Stretch 15 min	Squash game or practice or rest
Week 5	Stretch 15 min Run 5 mi (8 km) Strength 25 min Stretch 15 min	Squash game or practice	Stretch 15 min Run 2 mi (3.2 km) Jump rope 5 min Interval sprint 30 min Stretch 15 min	Squash game or practice	Rest	Stretch 15 min Ghosting 25 min Strength 25 min Stretch 15 min	Squash game or practice or rest
Week 6	Stretch 15 min Run 5 mi (8 km) Strength 25 min Stretch 15 min	Squash game or practice	Stretch 15 min Run 2 mi (3.2 km) Jump rope 5 min Shuttle run 20 min Stretch 15 min	Squash game or practice	Rest	Stretch 15 min Ghosting 25 min Strength 25 min Stretch 15 min	Squash game or practice or rest

OFF-SEASON CONDITIONING PROGRAM FOR THE TOURNAMENT-LEVEL PLAYER

The serious tournament-level player must dedicate some time in the off-season to conditioning. During the season, the player focuses primarily on tournaments and matches. Between tournaments and matches, the player should be practicing and resting. Trying to employ a vigorous conditioning program during the season likely will leave the player exhausted for important matches. Tournaments can involve several matches over a number of days. To stay fresh for a tournament, the tournament-level player should have a light practice session at the most on the two days preceding the event.

During the off-season, put together a schedule to work on all-around conditioning. Ideally, the program should be around eight weeks long (table 13.2) and, like the program for the recreational or club player, should start relatively easy and become more intense over time. Plan for five conditioning sessions per week. Each session should last an hour and a half to two hours. Schedule two or three additional sessions a week on court, playing or practicing.

Finish the conditioning program at least three weeks before the start of the season. Spend that period right before the season training on court with plenty of hard practice sessions to get your match play ready for the important games ahead.

Table 13.2 Off-Season Conditioning Program for the Tournament-Level Player

	Monday	Tuesday	Wednesday	Thursday	Friday	Saturday	Sunday
Week 1	Stretch 15 min Jump rope 5 min Ghosting 10 min Strength 30 min Run 1 mi (1.6 km) Stretch 15 min	Session 1: Stretch 15 min Jump rope 5 min Ghosting 10 min Shuttle run 10 min Run 3 mi (4.8 km) Stretch 15 min Session 2: Squash game or practice	Stretch 15 min Jump rope 5 min Ghosting 10 min Strength 30 min Run 1 mi (1.6 km) Stretch 15 min	Rest	Session 1: Stretch 15 min Jump rope 5 min Ghosting 10 min Interval sprint 10 min Run 3 mi (4.8 km) Stretch 15 min Session 2: Squash game or practice	Stretch 15 min Jump rope 5 min Ghosting 10 min Strength 30 min Run 1 mi (1.6 km) Stretch 15 min	Rest
Week 2	Stretch 15 min Jump rope 5 min Ghosting 15 min Strength 30 min Run 1 mi (1.6 km) Stretch 15 min	Session 1: Stretch 15 min Jump rope 5 min Ghosting 15 min Shuttle run 15 min Run 3 mi (4.8 km) Stretch 15 min Session 2: Squash game or practice	Stretch 15 min Jump rope 5 min Ghosting 15 min Strength 30 min Run 1 mi (1.6 km) Stretch 15 min	Rest	Session 1: Stretch 15 min Jump rope 5 min Ghosting 15 min Interval sprint 15 min Run 3 mi (4.8 km) Stretch 15 min Session 2: Squash game or practice	Stretch 15 min Jump rope 5 min Ghosting 15 min Strength 30 min Run 1 mi (1.6 km) Stretch 15 min	Rest
Week 3	Stretch 15 min Jump rope 5 min Ghosting 15 min Strength 30 min Run 2 mi (3.2 km) Stretch 15 min	Session 1: Stretch 15 min Jump rope 5 min Ghosting 15 min Shuttle run 15 min Run 4 mi (6.4 km) Stretch 15 min Session 2: Squash game or practice	Stretch 15 min Jump rope 5 min Ghosting 15 min Strength 30 min Run 2 mi (3.2 km) Stretch 15 min	Rest	Session 1: Stretch 15 min Jump rope 5 min Ghosting 15 min Interval sprint 15 min Run 4 mi (6.4 km) Stretch 15 min Session 2: Squash game or practice	Stretch 15 min Jump rope 5 min Ghosting 15 min Strength 30 min Run 2 mi (3.2 km) Stretch 15 min	Rest
Week 4	Stretch 15 min Jump rope 10 min Ghosting 15 min Strength 30 min Run 2 mi (3.2 km) Stretch 15 min	Session 1: Stretch 15 min Jump rope 10 min Ghosting 15 min Shuttle run 15 min Run 4 mi (6.4 km) Stretch 15 min Session 2: Squash game or practice	Stretch 15 min Jump rope 10 min Ghosting 15 min Strength 30 min Run 2 mi (3.2 km) Stretch 15 min	Rest	Session 1: Stretch 15 min Jump rope 10 min Ghosting 15 min Interval sprint 15 min Run 4 mi (6.4 km) Stretch 15 min Session 2: Squash game or practice	Stretch 15 min Jump rope 10 min Ghosting 15 min Strength 30 min Run 2 mi (3.2 km) Stretch 15 min	Rest

	Monday	Tuesday	Wednesday	Thursday	Friday	Saturday	Sunday
Week 5	Stretch 15 min Jump rope 10 min Ghosting 15 min Strength 40 min Run 2 mi (3.2 km) Stretch 15 min	Session 1: Stretch 15 min Jump rope 10 min Ghosting 15 min Shuttle run 15 min Run 4 mi (6.4 km) Stretch 15 min Session 2: Squash game or practice	Session 1: Stretch 15 min Jump rope 10 min Ghosting 15 min Strength 40 min Run 2 mi (3.2 km) Stretch 15 min Session 2: Squash game or practice	Rest	Stretch 15 min Jump rope 10 min Ghosting 15 min Interval sprint 15 min Run 4 mi (6.4 km) Stretch 15 min	Session 1: Stretch 15 min Jump rope 10 min Ghosting 15 min Strength 40 min Run 2 mi (3.2 km) Stretch 15 min Session 2: Squash game or practice	Rest
Week 6	Stretch 15 min Jump rope 10 min Ghosting 20 min Strength 40 min Run 2 mi (3.2 km) Stretch 15 min	Session 1: Stretch 15 min Jump rope 10 min Ghosting 20 min Shuttle run 15 min Run 4 mi (6.4 km) Stretch 15 min Session 2: Squash game or practice	Session 1: Stretch 15 min Jump rope 10 min Ghosting 20 min Strength 40 min Run 2 mi (3.2 km) Stretch 15 min Session 2: Squash game or practice	Rest	Stretch 15 min Jump rope 10 min Ghosting 20 min Interval sprint 15 min Run 4 mi (6.4 km) Stretch 15 min	Session 1: Stretch 15 min Jump rope 10 min Ghosting 20 min Strength 40 min Run 2 mi (3.2 km) Stretch 15 min Session 2: Squash game or practice	Rest
Week 7	Stretch 15 min Jump rope 10 min Ghosting 20 min Strength 40 min Run 3 mi (4.8 km) Stretch 15 min	Session 1: Stretch 15 min Jump rope 10 min Ghosting 20 min Shuttle run 15 min Run 5 mi (8 km) Stretch 15 min Session 2: Squash game or practice	Session 1: Stretch 15 min Jump rope 10 min Ghosting 20 min Strength 40 min Run 3 mi (4.8 km) Stretch 15 min Session 2: Squash game or practice	Rest	Stretch 15 min Jump rope 10 min Ghosting 20 min Interval sprint 15 min Run 5 mi (8 km) Stretch 15 min	Session 1: Stretch 15 min Jump rope 10 min Ghosting 20 min Strength 40 min Run 3 mi (4.8 km) Stretch 15 min Session 2: Squash game or practice	Rest
Week 8	Stretch 15 min Jump rope 10 min Ghosting 20 min Strength 40 min Run 3 mi (4.8 km) Stretch 15 min	Session 1: Stretch 15 min Jump rope 10 min Ghosting 20 min Shuttle run 20 min Run 5 mi (8 km) Stretch 15 min Session 2: Squash game or practice	Session 1: Stretch 15 min Jump rope 10 min Ghosting 20 min Strength 40 min Run 3 mi (4.8 km) Stretch 15 min Session 2: Squash game or practice	Rest	Stretch 15 min Jump rope 10 min Ghosting 20 min Interval sprint 20 min Run 5 mi (8 km) Stretch 15 min	Session 1: Stretch 15 min Jump rope 10 min Ghosting 20 min Strength 40 min Run 3 mi (4.8 km) Stretch 15 min Session 2: Squash game or practice	Rest

SUCCESS SUMMARY FOR CONDITIONING

It is very important for the serious player to dedicate some time away from playing and practicing to work on fitness. Squash players need to work on flexibility, speed, stamina, and strength. For every match, practice session, or conditioning workout, begin with a good warm-up and end with a cool-down. Include static and dynamic stretches that address each muscle group.

It is best to use the off-season to work on your conditioning. During the season you likely will be too busy with matches and tournaments to dedicate enough time to really improve fitness. Instead, find a period of the year when you have no matches and put together a six- to eight-week conditioning schedule. Start with relatively light sessions and then gradually increase the intensity of the sessions as you go through the program.

Congratulations on finishing the 13 steps to success. You are now ready to take the squash world by storm! Whether you began this program as a beginner or a more experienced squash player, you have learned the essential skills to improve your squash game. It is vitally important that you continually go back to work on drills from each of the steps because every player has room for improvement. With the right skills, squash is an exhilarating, fast-paced, mentally stimulating game. It is a great workout for people of all ages and provides a fun environment in which to exercise and compete with others. Most clubs offer ladders, leagues, and tournaments that enable players of all abilities to meet and play different people. Our hope is that you will derive years of enjoyment from playing the game.

Glossary

ace—A winning service when the receiver makes no contact with the ball.

all—A tie score; for example, 3-3 is "3 all."

American scoring—Another name for point-per-rally scoring; a scoring system in which games are played to 11, and points are scored regardless of who is serving.

angle—A shot that hits a side wall before hitting the front wall.

appeal—A player's request to the referee to allow a let or to reconsider a decision just made.

backcourt—The area of the court behind the short line.

backhand—A shot hit to the side of the body opposite the side on which the player holds the racket.

back quarter—The part of the court bounded by the side wall, back wall, half-court line, and short line. A served ball (if allowed by the receiver to bounce) must bounce within this area opposite the service box from which the ball was served.

backswing—The player's initial movement with the racket in preparation for hitting the ball.

back-wall boast—A shot hit against the back wall before hitting the front wall.

board—Another name for the tin, the area below the lowest horizontal line on the front wall.

boast—A shot that hits the side wall or the back wall before hitting the front wall.

British Open—A professional squash tournament in Britain; it was the unofficial world championship until 1976 and is still regarded by many players as the premier squash tournament.

carry—An illegal shot in which a player holds, or "carries," the ball on the racket strings.

choke up—To hold the racket higher, or closer to the racket face, on the racket handle.

conditioned game—A modified game in which the players can hit only certain shots or hit only to certain areas of the court.

consolation tournament—An event for first-round losers of a tournament.

crosscourt—A shot that lands in the opposite side of the court from which it was played.

deception—The act of setting up as if to play a particular shot but then hitting a different one in an attempt to wrong-foot the opponent.

default—When a player is awarded the match because the opponent fails to show up or is unable to compete.

die— A ball is said to die when it stays close to the floor after bouncing because a player hit it softly, with slice, or in the nick, thus making it impossible to return.

disguise—The act of setting up in such a way that the opponent is unable to tell what shot is going to be played.

double elimination—A tournament in which two losses eliminate a player or team.

down—The referee's call to indicate that the ball hit the tin or failed to reach the front wall.

down the line—Straight along the side wall.

drive—A basic forehand or backhand shot hit after the bounce to one of the back corners.

drop—A shot hit softly onto the front wall so that the ball dies in the frontcourt.

error—When a player loses a point due to a mistake (e.g., hitting the ball into the tin or out of court).

fault—An unsuccessful serve.

final—The last match of a tournament played to determine the winner.

follow-through—The final part of the racket's swing after the player makes contact with the ball.

foot fault—An unsuccessful service due to the server not having at least one foot completely in the service box when making contact with the ball.

forehand—A shot hit on the side of the body on which the player holds the racket.

game—Part of the match that is completed when one player scores 11 points in point-per-rally scoring or wins by 2 clear points if the score is tied at 10-10, or scores 9 points in traditional scoring, or wins the tie-break if the score is tied at 8-8.

game ball—The state of the score when one player will win the game by winning the next rally.

get—A successful return from a difficult position.

glass court—A portable court with one-way-view walls that can be erected in large halls to accommodate larger audiences.

grip—The way a player holds the racket.

half-court line—A line on the floor parallel to the side walls that divides the backcourt equally into two parts. The line meets the short line at its midpoint to form the T.

halftime—The referee's call to signal the midpoint of the warm-up.

half volley—A shot played close to the floor immediately after the ball has bounced.

hand—The duration of a player's time while serving.

hand out—The referee's call to indicate that a change of server has occurred.

International Squash Rackets Federation (ISRF)—The governing body for squash worldwide.

kill shot—A shot hit hard and low on the front wall so that it dies before the opponent has an opportunity to return it.

let—A situation in which a rally is replayed.

lob—A shot lofted high onto the front wall so that the ball arcs softly into the backcourt.

loose shot—A poor shot that bounces toward the middle of the court, giving the opponent a chance to hit a winner.

love—The term used for zero in the scoring system.

marker—The official who calls the score during a squash match.

match—A competition between two players; normally completed when one player wins three out of five games.

match ball—The state of the score when one player will win the match by winning the next rally.

nick—The crack between the wall and the floor. If the ball hits one of these cracks, it often rolls out, giving the player no opportunity to make a good return.

not up—The referee's call used to indicate that the player struck the ball after it bounced twice or that the player struck the ball twice.

out—An expression used to indicate that the ball struck a wall on or above the out line, struck the ceiling, or struck or passed through any fitting hanging from the ceiling.

out line—A continuous line formed by a horizontal line on the front wall 15 feet (4.6 m) above the floor, a horizontal line on the back wall 7 feet (2 m) above the floor, and diagonal lines on the side walls connecting the lines on the front and back walls. On courts with glass back walls, if there is no line on the back wall, the out line is considered to be the top of the glass.

penalty point—A situation in which a player wins a rally as a result of interference from the opponent.

Philadelphia—A shot played from the frontcourt. The ball is hit high on the front wall, near the corner, so that it hits the near side wall and then travels diagonally across the court to the opposite back corner.

point-per-rally scoring—A scoring system in which games are played to 11 points, and points are scored regardless of who serves.

professional—A player who makes a living from playing or teaching squash.

Professional Squash Association (PSA)—The organization responsible for running the professional squash tournament circuit.

racket face—The hitting surface, or strings, of the racket.

rackets—A game that is similar to squash but is played on a large slate court with a small, hard ball.

rail—Another name for a drive hit down the line.

rally—An exchange of shots beginning with the service and ending when the ball ceases to be in play.

receiver—The player who is not serving at the beginning of a rally.

referee—The official responsible for adjudicating all decisions during a squash match.

reverse angle—A shot hit against the side wall farthest from the striker of the shot.

round robin—A tournament in which a player or team plays against all the other players or teams. The winner is the player or team with the most wins.

server—The player who serves at the beginning of a rally.

service—The method by which a player puts the ball in play to begin a rally.

service box—The two squares on opposite sides of the court, just behind the short line, from which the server must serve.

service line—The middle horizontal line on the front wall 6 feet (1.8 m) above the floor. When serving, the player must hit the ball above this line.

set—The number of points the receiver chooses to play in a tie-break at the end of a game when using traditional scoring. If the score reaches 8-8, the receiver can choose set one and the game is played to 9, or set two and the game is played to 10.

short line—A line on the floor parallel to the front and back walls, 18 feet (5.5 m) from the front wall.

side (line) judges—Two officials who, in conjunction with the referee, are responsible for adjudicating decisions during a squash match.

single elimination—A tournament in which a loss eliminates a player or team.

skid boast—A shot hit from the backcourt. The ball is hit up on the side wall so that it strikes high in the center of the front wall and then travels to the opposite back corner.

slice—To hit the ball with spin (i.e., with an open racket face) so that the ball stays low after it hits the front wall.

stroke—Another term for shot. Also, another name for a penalty point.

sweet spot—The place on the racket face that produces the most power.

T—The line configuration in the middle of the court formed by the short line and the half-court line.

tie-break—In traditional scoring, the state of the game when the score reaches 8-8. The receiver must choose either set one and the game is played to 9 or set two and the game is played to 10.

tin—A metal strip 19 inches (48 cm) high at the bottom of the front wall (17 inches [43 cm] for professional matches).

traditional scoring—A scoring system in which games are played to 9 points, and only the server can score points.

trickle boast—A shot hit from the frontcourt that hits the side wall before hitting the front wall.

turning on the ball—A situation in which a player makes a 180-degree turn in the back of the court and hits the ball with the forehand on the backhand side, or vice versa.

volley—A shot hit before the ball has bounced on the floor.

warm-up—A 5-minute period before the start of a match to allow players to practice and to warm up the ball.

winner—A shot that the opponent cannot return.

wrong-foot—The act of forcing an opponent to move in a different direction from where the ball is going.

About the Authors

Philip Yarrow has been competing in and winning squash tournaments for almost 30 years. He was a member of the under-19 junior squad in his native England. While attending Nottingham University, he was both the English Universities and British Universities champion. His school's team won the English Universities Team Championship in all three years of his time there.

Philip moved to the United States in 1991 and won the National Amateur Championships in 1992 and 1993. At that time he was also building one of the best squash programs in the country as head squash professional at Chicago's Lakeshore Athletic Club. Philip is a certified coach with the English Squash Rackets Association, a certified referee in England and the United States, and a certified referee instructor in the United States.

Aidan Harrison has been heavily involved in squash since he first picked up a racket at the age of eight. Originally from Yorkshire, he captained the England under-19 junior team in 1990, which won the World Junior Team Championships, and he finished third that year in the individual event. Aidan turned professional at age 16 and played on the squash tour for five years, reaching the top 50 in the world rankings.

In 1993, he moved to Dallas to coach full time. He was head coach of the U.S. national junior women's team, leading it to a highest-ever fourth-place finish in the World Championships in 2001. At the same time, he was the personal coach to Michelle Quibell, who became the first American junior to win a British Open title. In 2002, he received the U.S. Olympic Squash Coach of the Year award.

Aidan is a certified coach with the English Squash Rackets Association, a certified Spinning instructor and a personal trainer. He is currently the head squash professional at the Onwentsia Club in Lake Forest, Illinois, one of the most prestigious country clubs in the United States.

STEPS TO SUCCESS SPORTS SERIES

The *Steps to Success Sports Series* is the most extensively researched and carefully developed set of book ever published for teaching and learning sports skills.

Each of the books offers a complete progression of skills, concepts and strategies that are carefully sequenced to optimize learning for students, teaching for sport-specific instructors and instructional program design techniques for future teachers.

The *Steps to Success Sports Series* includes:

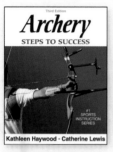
Archery — STEPS TO SUCCESS — Third Edition — Kathleen Haywood · Catherine Lewis

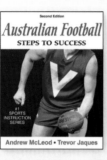
Australian Football — STEPS TO SUCCESS — Second Edition — Andrew McLeod · Trevor Jaques

Badminton — STEPS TO SUCCESS — Second Edition — Tony Grice

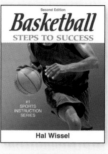
Basketball — STEPS TO SUCCESS — Second Edition — Hal Wissel

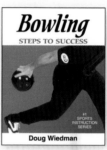
Bowling — STEPS TO SUCCESS — Second Edition — Doug Wiedman

Fencing — Steps to Success — ELAINE CHERIS

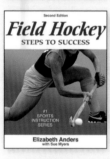
Field Hockey — STEPS TO SUCCESS — Second Edition — Elizabeth Anders with Sue Myers

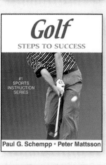
Golf — STEPS TO SUCCESS — Paul G. Schempp · Peter Mattsson

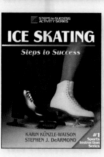
Ice Skating — Steps to Success — KARIN KÜNZLE-WATSON · STEPHEN J. DeARMOND

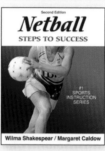
Netball — STEPS TO SUCCESS — Second Edition — Wilma Shakespear / Margaret Caldow

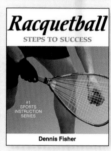
Racquetball — STEPS TO SUCCESS — Dennis Fisher

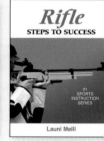
Rifle — STEPS TO SUCCESS — Launi Meili

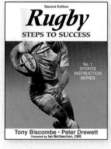
Rugby — STEPS TO SUCCESS — Second Edition — Tony Biscombe · Peter Drewett, Foreword by Ian McGeechan, OBE

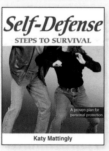
Self-Defense — STEPS TO SURVIVAL — Katy Mattingly

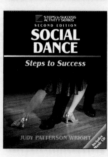
Soccer — STEPS TO SUCCESS — Joseph A. Luxbacher

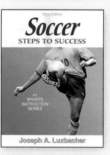
Social Dance — Steps to Success — Second Edition — JUDY PATTERSON WRIGHT

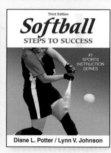
Softball — STEPS TO SUCCESS — Diane L. Potter / Lynn V. Johnson

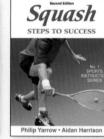
Squash — STEPS TO SUCCESS — Second Edition — Philip Yarrow · Aidan Harrison

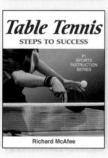
Swimming — STEPS TO SUCCESS — Third Edition — David Thomas

Table Tennis — STEPS TO SUCCESS — Richard McAfee

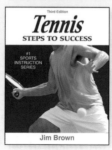
Team Handball — Steps to Success — REITA E. CLANTON · MARY PHYL DWIGHT

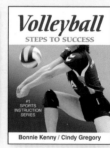
Tennis — STEPS TO SUCCESS — Third Edition — Jim Brown

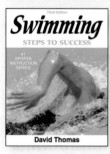
Volleyball — STEPS TO SUCCESS — Bonnie Kenny / Cindy Gregory

Weight Training — STEPS TO SUCCESS — Third Edition — Thomas R. Baechle · Roger W. Ear

To place your order, U.S. customers call
TOLL FREE **1-800-747-4457**
In Canada call 1-800-465-7301
In Australia call 08 8372 0999
In Europe call +44 (0) 113 255 5665
In New Zealand call 0800 222 062
or visit **www.HumanKinetics.com/StepstoSuccess**

HUMAN KINETICS
The Premier Publisher for Sports & Fitness
P.O. Box 5076, Champaign, IL 61825-5076

Second Edition

Squash

STEPS TO SUCCESS

Philip Yarrow
Aidan Harrison

HUMAN KINETICS

Library of Congress Cataloging-in-Publication Data

Yarrow, Philip, 1968-
  Squash : steps to success / Philip Yarrow, Aidan Harrison. -- 2nd ed.
    p. cm.
  ISBN-13: 978-0-7360-8001-9 (soft cover)
  ISBN-10: 0-7360-8001-5 (soft cover)
  1. Squash (Game) I. Harrison, Aidan, 1971- II. Title.
  GV1004.Y37 2009
  796.343--dc22

                              2009019886

ISBN-10: 0-7360-8001-5 (print)   ISBN-10: 0-7360-8626-9 (Adobe PDF)
ISBN-13: 978-0-7360-8001-9 (print)   ISBN-13: 978-0-7360-8626-4 (Adobe PDF)

Copyright © 2010, 1997 by Human Kinetics, Inc.

All rights reserved. Except for use in a review, the reproduction or utilization of this work in any form or by any electronic, mechanical, or other means, now known or hereafter invented, including xerography, photocopying, and recording, and in any information storage and retrieval system, is forbidden without the written permission of the publisher.

The Web addresses cited in this text were current as of August 2009, unless otherwise noted.

Acquisitions Editor: John Dickinson; **Developmental Editor:** Cynthia McEntire; **Assistant Editor:** Scott Hawkins; **Copyeditor:** Patsy Fortney; **Graphic Designer:** Nancy Rasmus; **Graphic Artist:** Francine Hamerski; **Cover Designer:** Keith Blomberg; **Photographer (cover):** Phil Cole/Getty Images; **Photographer (interior):** Neil Bernstein; **Visual Production Assistant:** Joyce Brumfield; **Photo Production Manager:** Jason Allen; **Art Manager:** Kelly Hendren; **Associate Art Manager:** Alan L. Wilborn; **Illustrator:** © Human Kinetics, Inc.; **Printer:** United Graphics

We thank the Onwentsia Club in Lake Forest, Illinois, for assistance in providing the location for the photo shoot for this book.

Human Kinetics books are available at special discounts for bulk purchase. Special editions or book excerpts can also be created to specification. For details, contact the Special Sales Manager at Human Kinetics.

Printed in the United States of America   10 9 8 7 6 5 4 3 2

The paper in this book is certified under a sustainable forestry program.

Human Kinetics
Web site: www.HumanKinetics.com

United States: Human Kinetics
P.O. Box 5076
Champaign, IL 61825-5076
800-747-4457
e-mail: humank@hkusa.com

Canada: Human Kinetics
475 Devonshire Road, Unit 100
Windsor, ON N8Y 2L5
800-465-7301 (in Canada only)
e-mail: info@hkcanada.com

Europe: Human Kinetics
107 Bradford Road
Stanningley
Leeds LS28 6AT, United Kingdom
+44 (0)113 255 5665
e-mail: hk@hkeurope.com

Australia: Human Kinetics
57A Price Avenue
Lower Mitcham, South Australia 5062
08 8372 0999
e-mail: info@hkaustralia.com

New Zealand: Human Kinetics
P.O. Box 80
Torrens Park, South Australia 5062
0800 222 062
e-mail: info@hknewzealand.com